P9-DEE-939

EFFECTIVE CHURCH SERIES

R. WADE PASCHAL, JR.
Edited by HERB MILLER

VITAL ADULT LEARNING

ABINGDON PRESS

Nashville

VITAL ADULT LEARNING
Choices to Fit Your Church

Copyright © 1994 by Abingdon Press

This book is printed on recycled, acid-free paper.

Library of Congress Cataloging-in-Publication Data

Paschal, R. Wade, 1951-
  Vital adult learning / R. Wade Paschal, Jr.
    p. cm.—(Effective church series)
  Includes bibliographical references.
  ISBN 0-687-00773-9 (recycled alk. paper)
  1. Christian education of adults. 2. Sunday schools. I. Title.
  II. Series.
  BV1488.P37   1994
  268'.434—dc20   93-28212
                                                                          CIP

Scripture quotations, unless otherwise noted, are from the New Revised
Standard Version of the Bible, copyright © 1989 by the Division of Christian
Education of the National Council of the Churches of Christ in the USA. Used
by permission.

94 95 96 97 98 99 00 01 02 03 — 10 9 8 7 6 5 4 3 2 1

MANUFACTURED IN THE UNITED STATES OF AMERICA

To all my teachers in the teaching ministry:

my wife, Sandi,
the teachers, classes, and staff of First United
Methodist Church Tulsa, Oklahoma,
and in memory of Dr. L. D. Thomas, Jr.

CONTENTS

FOREWORD

The Talmud tells the story of three scholars who were sent to inspect the quality of education across the Holy Land. In one community, they could locate no teachers. "Bring us the protectors of the town!" they demanded. Shortly, the local officials ushered in a group of military guards. "These are not the protectors of the town!" one of the scholars exclaimed. "The true protectors of the town are its teachers!"

Recent research indicates that this truth also applies to congregations. Transmitting the Christian faith to other persons requires more than effective preaching. Lifelong teaching and learning play major roles, too. Paul defined spiritual maturity as having the "mind of Christ" (1 Cor. 2:16). "Let the same mind be in you that was in Christ Jesus," he said (Phil. 2:5). Growth toward that kind of spirituality can begin in childhood but cannot reach full bloom if Bible study stops at age eighteen.

Early Christians were called disciples (learners), because they saw themselves as traveling toward a destination rather than having already arrived. Contemporary congregations that hold a similar view therefore place a strong emphasis on facilitating adult learning—a large percentage of which occurs in adult Sunday school classes. Wade Paschal provides the "nuts and bolts" for persons who intend to engage in adult learning with excellence. As well as benefiting teachers and adult disciples, these insights can strengthen the congregation's vitality. Many young adults believe strongly in Bible study. Churches that meet this need benefit both individual faith development and the congregation's overall ministry strength.

Paschal's leadership insights fit the goal of the Effective Church Series: to help meet the need for "how-to" answers in specific areas of church life. Each of these volumes provides clergy and laypersons with practical insights and methods that can increase their congregation's effectiveness in achieving God's purposes in every aspect of ministry: leadership, worship, Sunday school, membership care, biblical literacy, spiritual growth, small groups, evangelism, new-member assimilation, prayer, youth work, singles work, young-adult work, time management, stewardship, administration, community service, world mission, conflict resolution, and writing skills.

Paschal's insights also fit the theological focus of the Effective Church Series. While concentrating more on the practical "how to do it" than on the theoretical and conceptual, its "ideas that work" rest on biblical principles. Without that foundation, method sharing feeds us a diet of cotton candy—sweet but without nutrients. Paschal has addressed the subject of adult Christian learning in ways consistent with biblical truths and classic Christian theology.

Someone said that the universe is full of magical things, patiently waiting for our wits to grow sharper. Most pastors and adult education leaders—no matter how experienced—do not feel overqualified for their leadership roles. Avid learners themselves, they know that much beautiful scenery remains slightly beyond the horizon of their experiences and perceptions. By providing tall and practical insights, Paschal expands the view.

Herb Miller
Lubbock, Texas

I

WHO NEEDS ADULT CLASSES, ANYWAY?

The Asbury Class Sunday school class was established in 1923 as a young couples' class. Through the years the class had provided much of the leadership of the church. It had survived the Depression, world wars, police actions, booms and busts, and in 1983 was still strong enough to get about forty people together for class each Sunday. The church decided to honor the Asburians with a dinner, a picture, and a plaque. Most of the members were in their eighties and nineties at the time. Friends and church staff picked up class members from homes and nursing homes and managed to get together almost seventy Asburians for the occasion. It was a great time, and they all loved it. Within about five years the class had almost disappeared. Four or five people at most could make it on Sunday mornings, and they no longer had the energy even to take roll. The class disbanded, and those who could still make it to church joined other classes, where younger members were glad to take them in and care for them.

For sixty years the Asbury class provided much of the church's backbone. They taught Sunday school, went on trips with the youths, prepared the budget, directed the program, and made the church the church. They were also the backbone of one another's lives. They brought food in at times of birth and death. They shared anxiety as their children grew and left the house. They held one another as spouses died. They reminded one another that they were Christians trying to lead a Christian life, and they worked together toward that end.

Is this a way of life that is passing? Are adult Sunday school classes fading as the Asbury class faded?

Much of the world gets along fine without adult Sunday school classes. Sunday classes for adults seem to be a North American phenomena—more specifically in the central and southern parts of the country. Historically, Sunday schools for adults, as well as for children, were tied to a drive for literacy in the American frontier and among immigrant populations. People needed to read in order to be able to read the Bible, and this educational/evangelistic drive fueled the huge Sunday School Convention movement of the nineteenth century.

Literacy no longer drives adult education in churches. Social conventions that drew together church and clan have been splintered in our more mobile and modern society. Sunday school for adults seems to be a historical anachronism, or at best a time and place to drink coffee while the kids attend their classes.

Or is this really the case?

There is good evidence that a vigorous adult Sunday school program is integral to the spiritual and social health of Protestant churches today. Lyle Schaller notes adult education programs as an "almost universal characteristic" of growing and vital churches.[1] An intensive study by the Search Institute showed a strong correlation between church vitality and Sunday school program.[2] Those churches with strong adult Sunday schools seem to do a better job both of attracting and maintaining adult participation.[3] There is, in short, a growing body of evidence that supports the continuing importance of adult Sunday schools for the overall health of the church.

Why?

Just as one would think that we are getting past flannel boards and rap sessions, what is it that would get adults *back* into Sunday schools?

WHO NEEDS ADULT CLASSES, ANYWAY?

Believing, Belonging, Becoming

The vigor of adult classes and their importance for the church flows out of deeper, theological realities. Churches need adult Sunday school classes, or something like them, in order to fulfill what it means to be a church. Christian faith implies the transformation of people. In part, this comes from what we think and believe. In part, this comes through our relationships with other people that form and re-form us. In part, this comes from what we do.

A healthy church, and by implication healthy Christian individuals, needs a balanced diet of three things (and here I borrow from my friend and mentor, Dr. James B. Buskirk):[4]

Believing (*kerygma*—"proclamation"). We need, as individuals and as churches, to hear and respond to the spoken word of God. We need to be challenged at the level of heart and mind by God's Spirit and to have the opportunity to interact with that word. This is not just a personal response or individual piety, but a community response—we must be addressed as we relate to other people and respond in the context of these relationships.

Belonging (*koinonia*—"community"). The Christian life is lived in the context of community. The New Testament images of the church—such as the "body of Christ" (1 Cor. 12) and the "temple of God" (2 Cor. 6)—suggest the interconnection of individuals in the church. There is a sense in which we are not fully Christian until and unless we are in relationship with other Christians. We need the strengths of others to complement our strengths. We need the example of others to correct us. We need the encouragement of others not to give up. Without the protection and care of a social structure, the individual Christian faces many dangers: heresy, pride, self-deception, and despair. Community is absolutely essential for true Christian living.

Becoming (*diakonia*—"service"). Unless we participate in the servant life-style of Jesus, we have not fully incorporated the meaning of God's salvation in our lives. This is clearly one of the central themes in the Gospels (as we see it in John 13; Luke 22:28-32; Mark 10:42-45). While good works may not save

13

us, faith is not complete without concrete expression in Christian living (Eph. 2:8-10). It is a universal Christian experience that we grow as we put ourselves on the line for Christ. We need intentional and practical expressions of our faith in order for faith to move out of the realm of mind and emotions to become part of character and life-style. The balanced Christian life needs all three: a time to receive and respond to proclamation (*kerygma*); a time for fellowship and encouragement from other Christians (*koinonia*); and a time for service and expression of our faith (*diakonia*).

So, what does this have to do with the Sunday school class for adults? Rightly understood, adult classes can help meet our believing, belonging, and becoming needs in special and unique ways.

Believing

For a long time Lana came to class alone. Her husband was not hostile toward Christianity, but he seemed to feel that it was irrelevant. Several of the other men in the class approached him. They took him fishing and camping and did the sorts of things with him that he liked. He found out that these Christian men were not strange at all. In fact, the more he found out about them and the way they lived their lives, including the real questions and difficulties with which they struggled, the more he began to wonder about Christianity. Finally, he began coming to class, and then to church. He found a place in which it was acceptable to ask questions, a place where he could see the Christian faith being lived out. Lana probably could not tell you exactly when her husband made his own faith decision, but she knows where it happened—in the context of an adult Sunday school class.

We tend to connect *kerygma* most strongly with the preached word and corporate worship. This is correct, and Sunday school cannot replace corporate worship. There is a need for us as individuals, as Dietrich Bonhoeffer put it, to be silent before the Word of God.[5] We desperately need to take time to hear voices other than our own in life, and above all to allow space and silence when God's word addresses us. It is good for us not to be in control, to have to listen to a word from the outside. Sunday schools cannot replace the corporate act of worship for this very reason: classes tend to be times of dialogue and interaction on a peer level. Worship reminds us that we are not peers to God. When we miss worship we lose what we need most—the chance to be encountered and redirected by the word of God.

There is, however, an overlap between worship and adult learning in the growth of the "believing" part of faith. Believing is encouraged through both proclamation and dialogue. In a good adult class we hear the word of God taught and explained with the chance to interact and ask questions. Moreover, this is not just the chance for us as individuals to ask questions, but for us to hear the questions and responses of others. In the Sunday school class we get to see what is less obvious in worship—the reactions and interactions of others in the meaning of the Word for life. For example, the lesson may be about the way the Christian faith helps with suffering. This is a stimulating idea, and the teacher, perhaps working from Romans 5, develops Paul's thought in an interesting way. Then, someone comments that he found this to be true during a recent time when he was laid off and out of work. Another person responds by saying that she was in fact overcome by grief at one time, and she did not find it so easy to triumph in faith. The discussion has made the lesson extremely personal. The group is no longer talking about logic or correct thinking, but the truth that transforms their lives.

Preaching can do the same sort of thing in worship, but in the adult class you see the Word and the teaching of the Word interacting with the people you know. Your life and their lives and the reality of what is taught are on display for all to share and to see. It is one thing to hear something in a sermon, and quite another to know that what is said is being lived in a person you know.

It is also healthy to have a place where you can ask questions as well as hear. This procedure is not appropriate for the sermon (and not just because it reflects poor taste—theologically, we need to be challenged by the word before we ask questions)! But we do need to have our doubts and questions taken seriously. The Scripture seems to welcome this. Paul had many discussions in the synagogues, as did Jesus. Genuine seeking is always welcomed. John Wesley did not require conformity from those who came to his societies, but only the desire to "flee the wrath that is to come." People often spent a significant amount of time "seeking" before they became Christians in the Wesleyan societies—at times, as much as two years. This need to sort out and think through the issues is real and healthy, and adult classes can be a wonderful place for this to happen.

Belonging

Mike stood up in front of the class and began to thank those who had helped him and his family during the birth of their fourth child. When Mike and his wife went to the hospital, members of the class took their other three children and kept them during the birth. After the mother came home there was food on the table for several days and more help with the children. Mike ended his expression of gratitude by saying, "We can't imagine having a child without the help of our class!".

Studies have shown that somewhere between 75 and 90 percent of people who join a church already have a friend or family member who goes to that church.[6] One congregation did a study that confirmed this fact. They developed a long list of "prospects" for evangelism—people who were attending our church regularly but had not joined. The leaders discovered that all of the married couples and more than 75 percent of the singles on the list had already joined a Sunday school class. At that time, they were assimilating almost all of their new members first through Sunday schools by way of friendship and family networks. When the pastor checked the same list at another time, the situation was similar (although not quite so dramatic). Relationships are the major reason people come, or do not come, to church.

Adult classes are a primary means of encouraging and expanding relationships among Christians. In fact, the "belonging" function of a Sunday school class is even more powerful and important than its teaching function. Most of the images in Scripture emphasize the community nature of the faith. From the early tendency of the apostle Paul to go out with co-workers such as Barnabas, Timothy, and Silas, to the days of the Franciscans and the Wesleys and the modern small group movements, Christians have always found groups of some kind to be a normal part of the Christian life.

Why is this so?

We need help to translate what we know into action. We all know more than we do. While sometimes we fail through lack of knowledge, more often we fail because we lack the energy in ourselves to change. Dietrich Bonhoeffer wrote, "The Christian needs another Christian who speaks God's Word to him. He needs him again and again when he becomes uncertain and discouraged, for by himself he cannot help himself without belying the truth."[7] We can gain energy through others— through their encouragement, through their example and through the accountability we have through the group.[8]

As a pastor I began to notice a significant pattern among troubled marriages. In those that went on to divorce, there was always a "friend" who encouraged the person taking the action to go through with the divorce. This may have been a friend of the same sex or a friend of the opposite sex, but the constant was that this person encouraged the other by saying, "You deserve better. You've suffered enough. You're right to go after the other person."

Similarly, in the marriages that hung together through difficulties, there also had to be friends. These people, however, were telling the couple, "You can do it. Hang in there! This is worth saving. Can we take care of the kids while you two go work it out?" It would be too simplistic to say that these friends "caused" the outcome—there is no doubt that the people involved tended to choose that friend based on the outcome they were seeking. But it also became clear to me that in both cases, either in leaving or staying in the marriage, the people involved perceived a need to find strength and support in others in order to carry out their actions.

The expectations of others shape and effect our lives. When we see people who are important to us, who know us and care for us, their expectations for us reinforce our own goals and desires. It is always much easier to carry out a discipline if a group supports you. It is this power of mutual reinforcement that we get from others through their emotional support and help that makes fellowship so important in Christian living. Adult classes can and do provide significant fellowship and encouragement for Christian living.[9]

We need fellowship and community in order to meet a variety of personal needs. The McCommases had only come to class a couple of times when, while visiting for the church, they were in a tragic accident that left both husband and wife paralyzed. They had little or no insurance or resources, and now both were permanently and totally disabled. The Sunday school class rallied around them. Although they had very recently joined the class, for the next ten years (until the death of both) the class called them, visited them, cared for them, and raised literally thousands of dollars for their expenses. At the death of Bernice, the class mourned, because the act of caring had made it seem to them that they had not given as much as they had received.

No one person or family would have been able to meet the needs of the McCommas family. The whole class, sharing the burden together, was actually built up by the experience. What would have worn out even two or three families was a delight for the larger group.

We are not able, as individuals, to meet all the needs of people. Nor is it even healthy to try. If only a few are involved in meeting the needs of a person, then there is the danger of a proud or controlling paternalism on the part of the helpers, or a grudging dependency on the part of the helpee. If many are involved, then no one person can claim credit—the credit goes to Christ. Similarly, the person being helped can see the ministry received as the work of Christ through the church, rather than as a sign of personal failure or weakness. The caring is no longer a matter of special mercy to the person; but it becomes an extension of the total mercy of God in Christ in which all share.

This aspect of "belonging" in a Sunday school class can have some unsettling results for pastors. The pastoral staff of our church found the front line for pastoral care was really in the Sunday school. Often, the classes knew who was sick and hurting, and they were helping the people in need before the pastoral staff even knew what was happening. We learned to trust the members of our Sunday school classes about this and to rejoice over what they did. The pastoral staff depended on the classes to find out what was going on and what we could do to help. We saw that "pastoral care" was not just what the pastors did, but what the whole church did to care for those in need.

We are encouraged and molded by the examples of others. The easiest class to start is typically a newlywed class. The shock and thrill of this new relationship create tremendous needs in the new couples. They are re-forming their own relationship, often re-forming their circle of friends, and many times starting in a new place and in new circumstances. As a result, newlyweds especially enjoy being around other couples who are experiencing the same changes and stresses. They read together, share their successes and failures, socialize, and grow as couples. You might think that a newlywed couple would do well to spend time with older couples and learn from them. But older couples are generally dealing with other problems (transitions with children, parents, and job) and are no longer involved in a significant way with the issues that concern newlyweds.

So, the newlyweds find in one another the most significant and helpful models. And, biology working as it does, the cycle is repeated when they start their families and learn again from one another what it means to be young parents. Indeed, we learned it was time to form another newlywed class when young couples started complaining about hearing too many birth stories in class! When birth and early parenting transitions become more important than early marriage questions, the newlyweds no longer found the models they were seeking.

We are all looking for models to help us answer the questions confronting us in life, and we find these models in groups. In the computer age we have had a proliferation of "user groups" connected with various software packages. These are people who get together and share experiences using

19

the software with one another. This is a place to go and learn from others' hard-won experience and to share our own knowledge. Hearing the experiences of others not only teaches us how to solve our problems; it also encourages us not to be discouraged when new problems arise—there *are* solutions out there. The experience of the group reinforces our willingness to try.

This is equally true for Christians. We need models for living out our lives. We need people whose lives show us successes and the possibility of working things out. We also need the example of people who have failed and survived, reminding us that our failures are not God's final word about us. Adult classes, in their teaching, and even more in their social-relational function, address this need.

Becoming

In his journal John Wesley details this incident. The Methodists were called to help a family caught in illness. Wesley went to the house and found the husband dead, along with an infant child. The mother lay exhausted in her vomit, and of three living children, one had the strength to go and bring water to her mother. Wesley was so overcome by the pitiful sight that he (in his typical fashion) formed a program for the Methodists to visit the sick regularly.

Wesley divided London into twelve districts and asked for volunteers to visit, and where volunteers did not appear, he appointed visitors. One such man detailed in his journal his progress as a visitor. Having no idea what to do in visiting the sick, he looked through his *Book of Common Prayer*, and found a prayer for the sick there. This he used for about a year; then, he decided to write his own prayer. He used his own written prayer for a while, until finally in his journal he notes: "I have decided to pray without crutch," and he went on to describe how he finally felt free to pray extemporaneously with those whom he was visiting.[10]

We see here the connection between living our faith and growing in faith. What we know and believe is shaped and then reshaped by what we experience and do. Christian faith, above all, is not simply dogma and doctrine, but life. We experience our faith most vitally when we put it into action. Faith, as the epistle of James puts it, that is not expressed concretely is not faith at all (James 2:17).

Ministry or service to others is needed for a healthy and growing faith to stretch us beyond our own sense of comfort until we rely on God. The very relational nature of the Sunday school class makes the class sensitive to needs and individuals in ways that committees and boards often are not. The church as the body of Christ must look outward to maintain its existence. As Christ washed the feet of the disciples, we are to follow the Master's example (John 13:15). This is not an option or a good idea for churches. Service is part of our essence because the Christ whom we follow is a servant.

The key questions are: How do we stay sensitive to the needs of people? How do we motivate ourselves to service?

Needs that we know and see motivate us best. Needs that our friends know and see motivate us second best. Because classes know people, know their needs and hurts, and have resources for meeting these needs, they become a natural focus for ministry. Typically, classes focus on ministry which is personal and in which they have a real stake. They may not be very good at sending money "out there" to general needs. But they excel at feeding people they see need help, fixing houses they see broken down, and helping those they go to visit and touch.

My wife and I were visiting a class in another church on the day they discussed repairing the house of a very elderly woman confined to a wheelchair. The class fixed a fallen-in ceiling in the room where the woman spent most of her day, painted the walls, and put new curtains on the windows. The result for the woman was a much more cheerful and comfortable place to live.

The result for the class was just as significant. This was a new class, and the project drew them together. This experience made their faith less academic, more personal. They saw in clearer terms the meaning of Jesus' teachings about the poor, and they developed more compassion. This ministry was making the class, and the people in the class, something special.

Ministry and service were key means to spiritual vitality long before Sunday school classes came along. The offering of the early church was first and foremost gifts of food and clothing for the poor.[11] It was the hospitality of the Christians in the early church that largely set them apart from their culture. Renewal movements have frequently emphasized caring for the poor and needy as part of their renewal efforts (the Franciscans, the Methodist movement, the Salvation Army, and others).

Adult classes are, however, one of the most marvelous arenas for the concrete expression of the Christian faith. The thriving adult class will always have outreach opportunities that provide scope for intentional expressions of faith. Those expressions of faith in action will inevitably be the key points of class vitality.

When the pastor put out a call to help the church in Kenya, one couple volunteered to leave their jobs and home to go and organize the building project. They would be gone eighteen months, and their Sunday school class volunteered to pay their salary over those months—a commitment of over $18,000. Up to that point, the class (which averaged about forty in attendance) had never raised more than $3,000 in any year for missions. But, just as the couple felt called, the class felt the call to support them. So, they raised money, waited on tables at the local social organizations, did crafts, and gave sacrificially. They not only raised the money for "their" missionaries, but they also substantially remodeled the house of a single woman in need (who was not a member of the class).

After the missionaries came back, they held a class social. The social chaircouple went around the room introducing the class members, most of whom identified themselves by saying, "We joined the class since the Groves went on the mission field." This happened over and over, until finally they came to the missionaries who said, "We're the Groves!" During the time they were working so hard for "their missionaries" the class had almost doubled in attendance.

Numerical growth is not the only measurement of class vitality, much less of Christian maturity. Classes grow in other ways—spiritually, emotionally, and personally—but all these types of growth typically connect with some type of ministry and service.

Adult Classes and the Church

Adult classes do not define the church. But healthy churches need either healthy adult classes or something that takes the place of these classes (what that might be, we will discuss later). Every church needs to provide a place where the content of the gospel can be communicated, discussed, modeled, and experienced. Adult classes can do this well. Similarly, the church needs a place or experience in which people become connected with other people in community for support, example, exhortation, and care. Again, that is something adult classes do well. Finally, in order to grow, Christians must put their faith into action in meeting the needs of people in concrete fashion. This needs to be face-to-face ministry. And this is something that adult classes can do well.

Obviously, adult classes do not do these things well all the time. Starting an adult class is not a panacea for all ills. Churches exist with moribund adult classes. Particular adult classes may, in fact, *impede* all the above goals for church life. And there are churches that do many things quite well without adult classes. But adult classes, rightly used and guided, can be excellent tools for Christian growth and ministry.

This book will offer some ideas that make adult classes work in various kinds of churches. Your church will not be exactly like some of the churches we describe here. Going from the concepts and examples presented to your particular situation will demand some adapting and creativity. The results will be worth the effort. If adult classes make any sense for your church in its present situation (and there do exist situations in which typical Sunday morning classes do not make sense), then creating a healthy adult class program will pay many dividends for the life of your church.

II

THE GROWING BUSINESS OF ADULT LEARNING

When we recently moved to a small rural town, a newsletter from the local school district came among the first batches of mail. Alongside the announcements of new teachers and team schedules, the newsletter advertised classes for adults. Out of curiosity I counted the number of courses. This semirural county in Kentucky was offering a total of sixty-four classes for adults at one time!

These sixty-four classes illustrate the contemporary explosion of adult learning opportunities. In a metropolitan area people often have literally hundreds of options from which to choose. The public school system, the vocational training schools, community colleges, local universities, hospitals, private businesses, social agencies, government agencies, and *ad hoc* groups, provide instruction on a vast variety of topics and interests. These classes cover life issues ranging from minutiae to momentous—from learning about computers to cosmetics, from landscape gardening to literacy. Some of the courses are profound; some are not. Some are career related; some reflect personal interests. Together they reflect an enormous movement of time and resources into education for adults.

Several new realities fuel this increase in adult learning:

1. Modern life is constantly changing, and with these changes comes a need for updated skills and information.
2. People in our society have a democratic commitment to self-determination. Education is key to any sense of self-determination.
3. People are living longer. This gives a longer horizon for the use of skills and abilities. Many people have an increased yearning for education as they age. The expansion of higher education is essential for "second career" people at every age.
4. Education is a means for determining personal worth and values. These values are defined and redefined throughout life, leading to a continuing demand for educational opportunities.

With this expansion of adult education has come a similar growth in the professional study of adult learning. Huge amounts of money are spent for this education by individuals, businesses, and governments. Universities have developed programs in adult "andragogy" (as it is called), and there is an enormous body of professional literature. These people approach adult learning seriously and professionally.

The result is an ever-expanding web of educational opportunities for adults. These are usually quality programs targeting specific needs in adult lives. The educational opportunities that the church offers are often compared to these secular possibilities. People who come to our churches unconsciously ask: How good is your teaching and the education offered here? How will it help my life?

Modern theory and practice of adult learning raises some serious points for the church. The first is that we have some serious competition for people's time. Once upon a time the Wednesday night Bible study was pretty much the only show in town. The church was one of the few ongoing arenas for formal or semiformal education. The church is now merely one among an enormous range of options. The question is: Why should people come to the church at all for adult learning?

The explosion of adult learning opportunities and programs in North America should debunk the notion that business as usual in the church will be good enough for the future. All organizations naturally tend to focus services in terms of what they have done in the past. Organizations also tend to think in terms of the needs and comforts of the organization rather than the people being served.[1] Thus, churches often do what is familiar and comfortable rather than seeking to serve people. Because we have been doing Sunday school classes for so long, we may no longer even ask *why* we do them. It is simply what we have always done. Now we are forced to examine what we are doing in light of what is happening in adult learning in society at large.

Lessons from Adult Learning Theory and Practice

Adult learning has been a subject of scholarly research for much of this century. As in all the social sciences, adult learning specialists offer a variety of theories. This research does not always give us a completely clear picture of what the "real world" is like. Nor do these experts offer us one clearly "best way" for adults to learn. The professional material in this field does, however, offer the church some interesting insights. The following gleanings from this wide and rich field shed light on the church educator's challenging role.

The Adult Is Not a Child

Adult learners are not at all like children. While this fact is obvious, educators do not always act on it. In one sense in particular adults are different: they have experienced more of life. The nature of these experiences varies from person to person. But adults bring to the classroom their various transitions in life (from child to adult, student to worker, single to married and maybe back again, child to parent) and these experiences make their approach to learning and to thinking quite different from children.

26

1. Adults typically want their learning experiences to be connected with practical results.
2. Adults come to classes with a more specific sense of need. They frequently have particular problems or questions with which they want help.
3. Adults have more autonomy, more self-confidence, more of a sense of their own ability to participate in the process of learning than do children. They are often more inclined to question than children are, especially when their own experience is contradicted.
4. Adults come out of a much more complex world, with a variety of responsibilities stemming from work, home, and relationships.[2]

What does this mean in practical terms for the church? You cannot approach adult Sunday school classes as you do children's classes. Adults are probably going to be more demanding and more complex. They are going to ask, "So what?" They are going to process what they hear in a classroom through their own experience, accepting what "fits" and rejecting what does not fit. They will come when the teaching and material seem relevant to their lives, and they may well disappear when they judge the teaching to be irrelevant.

Adults come to class with their own expectations. Adult learning studies have stressed that most adults are involved in a class in order to achieve some sort of objective. Career and family are two of the major areas of interest.[3] However, research also shows that people often participate in adult learning experiences for reasons of personal satisfaction as well as for practical and economic goals.[4] The church will typically not be the first resource for people seeking to develop or enhance job skills (and maybe we miss an opportunity there). But the church is the natural place for people to turn when they are asking for direction in dealing with family issues and questions of personal meaning.

Adults in classes will be active and directed people. This audience is likely to be some of the most productive and busy people in society. The amount of leisure time is not related to interest in adult learning—just the opposite! Those with the least time are often the most interested in learning.[5] Women, younger people, single people, educated people, and affluent people are among those most likely to participate in adult learning.[6] This means that a congregation's leaders and workers will exert the highest demand for relevant and significant adult learning opportunities from their church (and will go where they can get these needs met).

In other words, adult learning theory and research tells us that we have a highly motivated group of people in our churches who are interested in learning. They will go to places where they can learn, and they expect to find resources for meeting their needs. The church can either respond to those needs or not. Not responding, however, will mean that we lose these people.

Adult learning should focus on the perceived needs of people. Any church, of course, wants to meet the needs of its people. But questions arise—What needs are we to meet? How do we decide what is a need and how to meet it?

Much adult learning theory begins with the well-known hierarchy of needs developed by Maslow:

* Physiological needs
* Safety needs
* The need to belong and be loved
* The need for self-esteem
* The need for self-actualization
* The need to know and to understand
* Aesthetic needs[7]

People have little motivation to learn until their basic physical needs of food, shelter, and safety are met. However, there is less evidence to support the theory that other needs really form the *hierarchy* that Maslow outlines.[8] That is, the attempt to see a progression from the need to belong to the need for self-esteem is probably misleading. All the so-called higher needs are apparent in individuals, without a great deal of differentiation. Needs do not actually stack one above the other in this neat, simple way.

What motivates most people to learn is a sense of disequilibrium—a sense of the possibility of more for their life. The disequilibrium may come from the changes that happen as we age, from problems in our families, or from a desire for personal growth or meaning. But people are most powerfully motivated to learn by the needs they perceive within themselves.

Knowing that people have needs and meeting those needs are two very different things. We have heard much of late about baby boomers coming back to church. Often, with the birth of the first child, young couples look for help in handling this new responsibility. They are aware of the difficulties of parenting, and they look to the church for guidance. Yet, evidence indicates that when boomers come back to church, they do not always stay long. Some come back and find little real help to handle this new pressure in their lives. They quickly conclude, "Church is as useless as I remember." The change in their life creates an opportunity for churches—but unless a church is ready to meet the need, the chance to reach these people soon disappears.[9] The church is once again dismissed and left behind, this time probably for good.

How do these insights apply to the church? Congregations who attempt to respond to the needs of people find that they have much which speaks to adults today:

1. The church is naturally a place of belonging, where people are accepted and loved in the grace of Jesus Christ.
2. The church gives meaning to life by lifting up the value of the individual in God's creation, and the meaning of life expressed through service, love, and justice. From the basis of God's work in Christ and in history, the gospel proclaims the meaning of persons.
3. The church in this sense speaks a directive and corrective word to people. We have been willing in the past to guide people in moral and ethical decisions and to provide examples for living.
4. The Christian faith has unique tools for speaking to adults. Part of the search for security is a need for standards and stability. The church has sources of authority and wisdom in the example of Jesus, the Scriptures, and the experience of the saints which speak in strength to the moral and personal questions of people today.

29

To a certain extent, many educators of adults would be a little uneasy with the above statements. The idea of an outside authority that directs and corrects the adult learner conflicts with a more democratic idea of teacher and learner helping each other to grow without imposing one's ideas on another.[10] Some adult educators prefer the term *facilitator* to *teacher* to emphasize that persons must learn for themselves, and we cannot impose knowledge from the outside.[11] Carl Rogers's work on client-centered practice has clearly influenced adult learning theory. The emphasis on a student-centered approach (much like client-centered therapy) suggests that to the greatest extent possible one wants to let individuals structure and organize their learning, promoting self-esteem and self-actualization for themselves.

The evidence allows us to both agree and disagree with that objection. Individuals are not always their own best guides—they can be trapped in their own world views and ignorance. They may need outside stimulus to break free from their past.[12] For example, in a racially segregated society a purely "student-directed" approach might do little to challenge the presumptions of the culture. Part of the church's reason for being is its responsibility to challenge, in the name of the gospel, the normal tendencies of individuals and cultures. The church at its best wants not only to affirm people, but to see transformation in the lives of people.

At the same time, a completely confrontational and challenging approach to people's needs may build in them a resistance that eliminates any chance of growth and grace. We must treat people with respect and honor their individuality—rather than browbeat or indoctrinate. The goal of Christian education is not conformity, but maturity—encouraging adults to focus their lives around Christ.

The Bottom Line

Adult educators are saying at least four important things to churches:

1. Focus on meeting the needs of people. This means we have to listen to our people and learn to respond to those needs.

2. Treat adults as adults. Make use of their experiences as people. Honor their individuality and make education a participatory event and not just the simple transfer of information
3. Deal seriously with the way faith offers meaning and strength in life's transitions. Speak from the authority of Christian revelation and tradition to the day-to-day needs of people.
4. Provide a context where people have value and identity. Adult classes should be the place where people are known as individuals and nurtured. Many of our needs for identity, self-esteem, and self-fulfillment are met when we are cared for in community and have the opportunity to care for others. Sunday school classes can be marvelous vehicles for just such experiences if we make use of them.

III

CLASSES HAVE PERSONALITIES

In Cambridge, England, stands a pub and stable once owned by a man named Hobson. Legend says that Hobson offered anyone who came to hire a horse the first animal available in his stable, and that one only. The expression "Hobson's choice" meant no choice at all. Nothing could be further from the expectations of people in our time.

Contrast this with a video produced by Centenary United Methodist Church in Lexington, Kentucky. The video pictures people of every age involved in a wide range of programs reaching college students, young singles, families, people going through divorce, and older people. This church had correctly identified its task: serve a broad range of people with a broad range of needs through a broad range of programs.

People, Stages, and Generations

This is the age of mass customization. The typical food store offers tens of thousands of product choices. The most popular stores offer a combination of products: foods, household items, flowers, and fresh baked goods. People want convenience, price, and choice in abundance.[1] The evidence suggests that modern adults are looking for places where a variety of needs can be met, and met well.

How can the local church understand the variety of needs and desires represented among adults? This bewildering task becomes easier if we break the subject down into the issues of personality and life cycle. Personality means that people are different. Some are outgoing and some are not. Some are natural leaders, some prefer to follow. As people differ in personality, so do adult classes. The personality of a class is complex (being made up of many people), but people who have similar tastes and attitudes tend to get together in social groups. This grouping process tends to give each class a general personality reflecting the majority of the personalities that make up the class.

People also go through reasonably predictable changes as they age. Part of this change involves certain basic events—college graduation, marriage, first job, first child, and so on. These events happen for most people within a fairly narrow age range. Beyond this reaction to basic events are more fundamental changes in outlook and attitude that come with age. When we are young, for example, most of us believe we have a range of options in life. But as we go along and make decisions, we realize that each decision begins to limit our future options. When we choose a major in college, this means *not* majoring in other subjects. Getting married means not being in the same types of relationships we had before marriage. Living in one place means not being elsewhere. Coming to grips with the necessity of limits leads us to view ourselves and our lives differently. This has positive and negative results in different people, but it is an inevitable part of growing.

In other words, as people age, they change. They change the questions they are asking, and the motivations that empower their decisions. Because of the tendency for like to choose like in organizations, many classes (though not all) will travel through these life cycles together.[2] You cannot, therefore, offer the same fare and the same treatment to different classes and expect a good response. Good adult learning allows for as many differences as possible. You cannot have a class or a course for each and every individual need. But you can figure out the larger needs suggested by the different personalities of people and classes, and the different stages in life cycles. Then, you adapt your teaching and curriculum to these special needs.

Personalities

I became convinced that the Boomers Class had potential for growth. The class was the right age—basically, baby boomers. All of the class members were involved in various ministries of the church; therefore, I was convinced the class had committed Christians as leaders. They were educated and basically nice people. Their room was small and not too easy to find, so it seemed to me that with a few changes, we should see instant growth.

We moved the class to a more accessible location with more room. I began to send my very best teachers to the class to teach. With the people they had, the room, and the teachers, growth would surely come naturally. We waited and watched. Over a period of years, very little growth happened.

For a long time I was stumped by the Boomers Class. Was I wrong about their commitment as Christians? I visited many of them in their homes, watched them around the church, and there was no doubt in my mind that as a class the Boomers were above average in their commitment and participation. They cared deeply about their faith and were definitely active in their expression of that faith. It wasn't their commitment, or the location, or the teachers that made the difference. It was their personality.

The Boomers were essentially a quiet group of people. They were nice but not outgoing. They had become good friends through the slow familiarity of years. Because they were all basically quiet, serious people, they felt comfortable together. They certainly welcomed anyone who came to class, but only those who were similarly quiet and reserved felt at ease there. Almost no one in the class was outgoing and gregarious enough to draw significant numbers of new people into the class and make them feel at home. Other classes did, and these classes tended to grow.

This analysis does not mean that the Boomers were in any sense a disappointment or a failure. Quite the opposite—they were and are a great class of caring people. They simply taught me that classes have personalities just as people have personalities. If you work with and understand these personalities, you will make better decisions than if you treat all classes as if they were alike. You cannot punch certain buttons and watch the desired result pop out like an answer from a calculator. Adult classes, like all human institutions, are more complicated than that.

Classifying Class Personalities

Different authorities define classes in different ways. No one way is perfect. All systems run the risk of overgeneralization. But some reflect more common sense than others. Warren Hartman illustrates one of the better ways in his fine book *Five Audiences*. Here, he outlines five types of classes. His division of these personalities represents a statistical, sociological approach emphasizing groups that share common demographic contexts and common outlooks. This very useful approach in some ways parallels the typology we will use.

An alternative approach might be to work from psychological or motivational categories. The manner in which Myers-Briggs personality type inventories apply to individuals, for example, may have some relevance to groups.[3] I will suggest seven types of classes, recognizing the somewhat arbitrary nature of any schema.[4] There will always be some people in a class who do not fit the overall pattern. Some classes will have characteristics that fit into several "types." Nevertheless, class personalities, like individual personalities, can be roughly typed according to dominant characteristics. The value of the process lies in learning to recognize the particular needs of various groups and to respond to those needs appropriately.

The Introverted Class is the shy, more reserved class. Often the class members work in occupations that do not require a high level of personal interaction (accountants, engineers, and so forth). They tend to form relationships less vigorously, but not necessarily less deeply. They tend to react quietly to new people, not out of suspicion or dislike, but out of natural reserve.

Introverted classes add new people leisurely, and typically attract persons who like this slow process. Being quiet does not mean that they do not have strong commitments—they may be highly involved in many ways. But typically, you see their involvement sometime after it happens. They do not make a big deal of what they do.

Some Ideas: These classes will appreciate outgoing teachers, but not overly aggressive teachers. They want to make strong, lasting relationships and will respond to teaching and projects that promote this. They will respond best to approaches that allow them to process and reflect on ideas and goals rather than asking for immediate responses. If you intend to use a discussion format, you will need a strong leader who can encourage and draw out conversation. When you seek input from members, be prepared to listen seriously. Input they volunteer probably reflects deep feeling from the class.

The Extroverted/Social Class is lively and talkative. Members may overwhelm new people with questions and attention when they walk through the door. Many of the class members exude energy and humor—maybe too much humor for some visitors. They enjoy meeting together and developing their social network. The extroverted class is excellent at welcoming people, but may not be as good at listening to and absorbing new people. Members seem noisy and pushy to some who attend, but they mean well in their enthusiasm.[5]

Some Ideas: The class will enjoy relational teachers and opportunities for social mixing. Members will do projects on the basis of getting together to be with one another, and less on the basis of what needs to get done. Topics that deal with relationships and teachers who are very personal will do well in this class. Rote teaching or teaching that fails to invite their participation will not do as well. They may need leadership in developing the ability to reflect and meditate.

The Missions/Service Class puts its emphasis on doing. Its life is oriented around projects, typically for others. The class may put a great deal of emphasis on raising money for these projects, or it may do a great many repair and restoration projects for people. The class will typically have a strong foreign missions support emphasis, a strong commitment to local service to the poor, or both. This group impresses those who like action and practical Christianity.[6]

The class may not be as strong in terms of caring for the social needs of its own people. Functions just for fun and being together may be few and far apart (and even then combined with some good work project). The group will seem overly serious to some people, and maybe a bit overdemanding.

Some Ideas: Missions class members are more concerned with the character of their teacher than the teacher's ability to communicate or the content of the lesson.[7] They receive instruction best from teachers who present lessons that are clearly practical and service oriented. At the same time, anything that helps the class focus on relationships strengthens the class in the long run. Planning retreats or social functions helps round out the class personality.

The Leader Class contains many people who naturally gravitate to leadership positions in the church. The class frequently comes up with new projects, ideas and functions. They are people who find ways to put those ideas into action. Members of the group gravitate to the forefront of whatever is happening in the church, and they expect to have a significant say in what happens. In many cases, the key leaders of the church will congregate in a few classes, or possibly even one class. From that class they foment much of the thinking/action muscle in the church as a whole.

If the Leader class is all leaders and no followers, it may have a problem. Leaders often want to delegate much of the work, and without someone to whom they can delegate, the class may struggle. The class may develop a reputation of being overbearing and arrogant, although this may not be at all fair or true. The people in the class may not intend to dominate the church; many in the class are just naturally accustomed to thinking and leading.

Some Ideas: Leader classes like courses and teachers that emphasize vision and progress and the "big picture." The class will probably want to participate in the lesson through discussion. Only an unusually strong teacher can get by with pure lecture, and only a strong person can handle the class discussion. People in the Leader class often become impatient with too much detail in a lesson. The group may need the balance of coming down out of the "big picture" to focus on individual needs and concerns.

The Supportive Class forms itself primarily out of those people who do not see themselves as leaders. The Supportive class is willing to work and act as long as someone else gets up front. These are people who want to serve, but not be seen. Some people do not feel comfortable in the dominant atmosphere of the Leader class, but prefer to be around "just folks." Supportive classes are willing to be positive participators without having to initiate the ideas. Still, a Supportive class wants the right to comment on what happens and offer their approval. Because of this trait, the Supportive class may tend to react and be negative. While they do not want to lead, they do not want to be run over, either. They expect to be consulted and to have their say and are hurt if they do not. Without a few leaders in the class, it may fall apart due to lack of direction. At the extreme, one disaffected leader who does not fit into the regular Leader class may take over a group of supporters and make it a negative weight, attacking the ideas of the leaders in the church.

Some Ideas: Like the Leader class, Supporters enjoy teachers and courses that focus on vision and mission, but they also will want a sense that individuals are important. They respond to practical applications of their faith in much the same way as the Missions class, except less aggressively. They will place a high premium on inclusive practices and democracy.

The Experimenter Class is like the Leader class in that the members like new and visionary ideas. However, they may not be leaders as such, but people who enjoy innovation and change. Whereas the Leader class wants to go someplace, the Experimenter class wants to go someplace *new*.

Whether the class is charismatic in worship or liberal in theology, it will be known (and enjoy being known) as the class that is different in the sense of breaking away from the norm. The class may lack stability if it tries too many new things. Similarly, it may become so tied up in its image of being different that it may react, on principle, to anything that everyone else is doing. Thus these people may not readily accept what is being done by the church as a whole, but they may want to put their own twist on everything that happens.

Some Ideas: This class will enjoy being challenged and confronted with creative ideas (in fact, this is a must). The members will want to participate in lessons through discussion. They will respond to creative and outgoing teachers. The key skill will be finding ways to link the class with the church as a whole without stifling its innovative personality. This can be done through including the class early on in the planning stages, and working closely with the class leadership.

The Traditionalist Class is conformist. The members value what they have always known and approach change skeptically, if not negatively. They want order and tradition, and they offer security and peace to those who have a clear idea of how church was in their past and liked it that way. The Traditionalist class keeps the value of its past alive and working for the church. The class members often stress loyalty to the church as a cardinal virtue.

The Traditionalist class typically enjoys biblical teaching and lecture formats.[8] It will accept change if it is part of consensus direction of the church—in short if innovations reflect a loyal support of church programs, this group will be supportive.

We tend to think of Traditionalist classes as older age-range classes, but that is not always the case. Younger classes may have Traditionalist leanings in the sense of a commitment to biblical study and traditional values. However, the difference between these types of Traditionalist classes reflects generational values. Older Traditionalists support the church because they value institutional loyalty. For them, their faith is synonymous with the church. Younger Traditionalists have little institutional loyalty. They probably came to faith outside the denomination through a parachurch organization. They are loyal to what they believe first, and then to the church insofar as the church supports that belief system.

Some Ideas: Honoring the beliefs and values of this group is important, but that does not mean capitulating to everything. Members of this class receive teaching when it is biblically based and when it appeals to their basic value system and to their sense of order and justice. A well-prepared and respected teacher will get a hearing from them—even for new ideas, if she or he establishes an accepted basis for authority.[9]

A Pastor Who Understood Class Personalities

When the charismatic movement hit many mainline churches, the result was often a church split. At the head of the resistance to these new and zealous Christians were many Traditionalist classes. But in the church where I was a staff member this never happened. As I studied its history, the reason became clear. The pastor had carefully developed a biblical approach to spiritual gifts that honored both the charismatic and noncharismatic positions. He next developed a course taught by respected leaders of the church. This combination of a biblical approach taught by respected leaders was enough to gain tolerance and understanding from both sides, and in the end an appreciation for the contributions of both. The pastor intuitively understood the personalities of the classes and leaders involved, and he dealt with the challenge by appealing to each group in a manner by which they could best receive his point.

Applying this concept. Each personality has its strengths and weaknesses. And, to some extent, most classes are something of a mixture of the above "types." None of the twenty-three classes in the church where I worked fit perfectly any of the above types. Some were more than one type. Some classes changed their personality as times changed and as people came and moved away. Yet, asking the question "What is the personality of this class?" helped us approach each class more appropriately.

Thus, if I wanted our adult classes to grow and open them up for new people joining the church, I needed to do more than move the Boomers to a larger classroom and give them good teachers. If the class and I agreed on growth as a goal for them, then we needed to work on ways to welcome new people more easily. Achieving that objective would depend to a great extent on the class personality.

Similarly, if we were considering a new idea or project, then obviously we needed to get the Leader classes on board. But this did not mean that we could afford to ignore the Supportive classes—they needed the chance to think about the idea and check off on it, too. The Leader classes gave energy and vision to an idea, and the Supportive classes provided muscle and time.

We also knew that our Missions classes would not be satisfied without some mission/service emphasis in the curriculum. And we planned flexibility into the courses for the Experimenters. Some classes needed a teacher strong on lecturing; others demanded someone with good discussion skills. The key was to connect interest, personality, courses, and teachers as much as possible.

Is there a danger in all this "class typing"? Of course! We could thereby put a class in a categorical box and ignore the real complexities of each group. But that danger is no greater—and, indeed, I think it is less—than the danger of trying to treat everyone alike when they are not alike.

Ages and Stages

Along with the basic personality types noted above, we must also be aware of the various stages of life that people, and therefore classes, go through. A person does not become an adult at age twenty-one and stop growing or changing. People go through tremendous changes in personality, goals, and values through the whole of life. Some of this is related to the normal events of adult life: marriage, birth of children, job changes, departure of children, health changes, and the approach of death. Along with this are changes in values and outlook that reflect the adult growth process.

We can view this process in many ways. Some studies have suggested as many as nine cycles in the adult growth process,[10] while others see three or four.[11] For our purposes, I have summarized six stages of adult growth and transition.

The Early Twenties—Independence. At this stage young adults are separating from their parents and establishing their own sense of identity. In the early twenties separation and independence from family are the dominant issues. This is why marriages begun before age twenty-three are more likely to fail than marriages begun between ages twenty-three and twenty-nine.[12] Many of these early marriages come out of an unconscious need to separate from parents before the individuals develop a fuller sense of who they are and what their goals are. Whether married or single, younger adults are most interested in distancing themselves from their parents and establishing their own ways. The adult class for this group has to honor that independence.

At the same time, younger adults throughout their twenties and thirties are looking for mentors.[13] They are looking for older adults (not their parents) who can guide and nurture their dreams and goals without controlling them. Our "college" class enjoyed having a leader slightly older than themselves who performed this role. Classes a little older than the collegians enjoyed having key "elder" figures in the church relate to them but not in direct leadership positions. They wanted guides and models, but they were their own leaders.

Late Twenties—Establishment and Intimacy. The late twenties are still a time of testing options and keeping life possibilities open. At the same time, people are beginning to move toward closure on certain basic issues. They are probably in a job they think of as a serious career possibility. They are probably finalizing their marriage commitment with a person. The late twenties is a time of making choices.

Most people at this time are sufficiently independent from their parents that they are not asking, "How am I different from my family?" as much as "Who do I think I am, really?" They are developing life plans and goals and basic principles for their early family and career life.[14] Not surprisingly, these classes devour information on basic family goals and values, career orientation, and meaning for life. They are looking to set the vision for life, and they are eager to receive Christian guidance.

Early Thirties—Settling Down. By the early thirties, most adults have made some basic decisions and are "settling down" to get on with life. They are raising children and struggling to advance up the career ladder. Researchers who follow groups as they mature have noted with surprise the conventionality of people in their early thirties.[15] But this is largely because this group has made a set of basic choices and is working them out.

These are times of rapid change for a Sunday school class. Along with many births, members will also move frequently as promotions and job changes come along. People may buy their first house or move into a larger one. With the demands of career and young families, this is an extremely busy time—possibly busy enough to curtail deep inner reflection.

These classes typically want reinforcement from the church. They want help in raising children, keeping their marriage communication going, and a lift to their spirits as their strength is drained. These classes are often delighted by missions projects that lift them out of their own world. The change of perspective is refreshing as well as challenging. At the same time, they are naturally drawn to family-oriented projects, such as working with orphanages and youth projects.

Mid-life—Appraisal and Renewal. There is more speculation than agreement regarding *when* mid-life begins and ends and what it means. The term *mid-life crisis* has become a cliché. Some researchers suggest that although many people experience much transition and reappraisal in mid-life, the incidence of cataclysmic crisis is not large.[16]

Mid-life is generally defined as that period of life between about thirty-five to about fifty. During this time we are confronted by the results of our earlier decisions. We realize that as we have chosen one way we have eliminated other options and so have limited our lives. We are forced to accept the fact that we cannot do all things, but only some things. Some original dreams have to be modified—either because we realize that we were hopelessly unrealistic, or more sadly, because we have lost hope.

We begin to realize that life is limited, too. This may happen as we see our parents or our friends' parents die. Or we will begin to lose a few of our contemporaries to sickness as well as to accident. In any case the realization that we are not going to live forever and that we are not going to be able to accomplish everything leads us to ask, "What do I really want my life to count for? What is the reason I am here?"

Classes composed of people in this age group want more complex and sophisticated answers than others. They have experienced ups and downs in life, and they realize that life does not always reward hard work and integrity in a fair fashion. If those in their twenties are looking for a path and a way, those in mid-life are wondering about the rocks in the path.

The mid-life class is not looking to the church for easy answers so much as for hope, strength, and encouragement. These persons will appreciate realism and honesty and integrity. They are getting past their need for mentors, but they are ready for some honest self-examination and restructuring of their lives.[17]

The Fifties—Giving and Creating. By their fifties people tend to become more comfortable with what they have become. Most adults have come to grips with what they can do and what they will not be able to do. In many cases people are becoming grandparents. They have achieved some recognition and satisfaction in career or family or at church.

Typically, these classes want to be giving and involved. The members are probably at their height of leadership potential in the church. They finally have time for projects outside family and work. Depending on the college status of their children, they may even have money.

Much like the younger couples in their thirties, this group is primarily seeking reinforcement of their basic values and goals. However, because they have been through the wars in life and have suffered, they are not so inwardly focused and tied to their own family and career. They will enjoy experiences and teaching that deepens and widens who they are and what they think.

Retirement Adults. With the improvement in health care and diet, people are living longer and with more vitality. As people approach retirement they are finding that they have more than a decade after they stop working when they will be generally in good health and have abundant energy. "Old age" does not begin at age sixty-five, but more like age eighty-five. Thus many classes of people aged sixty-five and up are extremely active and enthusiastic.

As time goes on, of course, these classes must deal with problems of health and the loss of a spouse. They will focus a good deal of their energy on caring for one another in these situations. This caring fellowship is the heart of their Sunday school and church experience.

They will enjoy good teaching as much for the personality of the teacher as for the content. They are probably serious about their faith and open to good study. But their searching for answers is not the same as the searching of younger people. Most basic issues have long been settled. This is not to say that there is no growth or development among retirement-age people. One retirement couple went to Costa Rica and served three years as missionaries, learning Spanish and adding a whole new dimension to their lives. Another widow became deeply involved in spiritual development, attending classes at a monastery. She developed significant insights into spiritual formation and taught courses on this to others. Each of these senior adults explored aspects of their faith to new depths and applications, and this is not atypical for people in retirement.

Using Ages and Stages

The purpose in outlining these stages of adult growth is not to typecast classes, but to point out the changing needs of adult classes. A church uses two key tools to meet these needs: curriculum and teachers.

You want to focus your curriculum around the needs of the individual classes. Younger classes, for example, will be inter-

45

ested in material that helps them in their marriages, as parents, and in setting basic life goals. Members of mid-life classes will be wrestling with a different set of family issues: they will be dealing with adolescents and with the change going on in themselves and their spouses. They will want to wrestle with the problems of life's limits and their own imperfections. Older adults will have little use for family-life topics—except for brief teachings on grandparenting. They will want to go deeper into their faith and be offered new opportunities for application.

You also meet needs, however, through the personality and characteristics of the teachers. Good teachers apply the content of the same basic courses differently to the needs of the classes they teach. A course on the Gospel of John might focus on faith as a life-direction decision for a younger class and a life-encouraging decision for a mid-life class. The key is finding teachers who respond sensitively to the different questions each class needs to address.

Trying to match a teacher's personality or characteristics with the needs of the class may reap huge dividends. If possible, assign people with mentoring skills to teach younger adult classes whose members are looking for mentors. The Traditionalist class will respond best to a Bible teacher they see as a respected Christian. Missions classes will look for a teacher who is an example they can follow. As the teachers adapt to the needs of the group, your classes will respond with increased enthusiasm.

Churches that try to recognize what is going on in the lives of their adults, and then organize teachers and curriculum to respond to those needs, will energize life in their classes. Classes are probably going to organize around similar personalities and points in the life cycle. They will therefore be strengthened if the teaching reinforces that organizing principle, rather than ignoring it.

IV

FORMING NEW ADULT CLASSES

Jack and Joan have just married and are thrilled with the prospect of their new life, but they are not quite sure how to fit into the church. They go back to their singles class, but their old friends mainly talk about their jobs, who they are dating, or what trip they will take next. Somehow, those topics are not so critical for Jack and Joan right now. They go to the old newlywed class, but they complain to the pastor, "Gee, preacher. Everyone there is having babies. The teaching was all about the influence of TV on children. What does that have to do with us?"

Jack and Joan present not a problem but an opportunity to their church. Starting new classes means finding needs and creating a format for fulfilling them. New classes in your church will best form among people who have not found a niche in one of your present classes and with their network of friends. If you survey the unmet needs of people in your church, most will fall in one of two basic types: people in a transition point of life or people with special needs or interests.

The transition points in life provide the impetus for forming new relationships. New adult classes therefore often spring from people who are looking for help and encouragement in facing some life-changing situation. Persons who are newly married, newly widowed, just divorced, recently starting a career, or just moved into town are people who are forming new relationships and dealing with new life problems. These twin needs offer opportunities to create adult classes.

People with special needs and interests may not be involved in existing classes. Families with special needs children often do not have exactly the same interests as other families. They therefore find strength in being around other families in similar situations. The single parent may not feel that either the typical singles class or the typical married couples class "fits." Young, blue-collar couples may not feel entirely at home in some adult classes. If one of these people came into your church, where would he or she find a group attuned to his or her questions and needs? If you cannot come up with a quick answer, you may have potential for forming a new class.

The easiest class to start is the one for newlyweds. We typically started a newlywed class about every two or three years. The adjustment to marriage dominates the world of the newlywed. Couples struggle to define their relationship and to redefine themselves at the beginning of marriage. At the same time, their friendship network changes after marriage—they no longer have the same goals in relationships as their single friends do. If the church offers them help in understanding the dynamics of their new relationship, and a structure for forming new friendships (especially with people asking the same questions), couples will participate in a newlywed class.

Starting the new class requires recognizing the special questions relating to marriage being asked by this group and the special friendship needs of new couples. A new class offering *content* related to newlyweds' questions and the opportunity for *relationships* with similar couples will attract newlywed couples. If you can combine a learning need and a relational need, you have the best possible combination for new adult classes.

Begin new classes by looking carefully at the memberhip of the classes you have now. *Who is not there?* A good goal for a Sunday school program is to have an average adult Sunday school attendance of about 50 to 55 percent of your adult *sanctuary attendance.* That is, if you are averaging 100 *adults* in your worship service, you could anticipate having 50 to 55 adults on average in Sunday school. If you are averaging less than 50 percent of your average adult worship attendance, new groups could probably be pulled together.

The following questions will help to locate potential members for new classes:

1. Check your classes for age and population distribution. What age levels are unrepresented? Does the church have any other worship attenders in this age group? If so, you might be able to gather some of them for a class.
2. Check your church leaders—are any unattached to a class? Some may simply prefer not to go to a class, but others may be available to help form a nucleus of a class from people they know.
3. Have people dropped out of a class? This probably reflects some personal search or need that is not being met. Talk with these people and see if there are enough with similar needs to form the focus of a new class.
4. Are there other kinds of groups (other than age groups) who are not finding a place in any class? One church found that their charismatic members were floating from class to class. A few of these people agreed to form the core leadership for a new class built around an emphasis on worship and music that appealed to them. Growth was slow, but within a few years, the class grew until it was the second or third largest class in the church.
5. Is there a group in the community to which you would like to reach out? Look for community groups that are not being served in a church and take time to get to know some of these people. This may mean reaching out to a different kind of people, but it could add breadth, growth, and depth to your church.
6. Listen attentively to any expressed needs in the church. When people say, "Gee, I wish I had a group of single parents to share with," they are helping you identify potential need groups. Ask, "Okay, who do you know

49

that might come?" If you can write down six to eight names, you have identified a potential need.

Form a Nucleus

Once you identify a need, next invite those people to meet with the adult education leader who best fits that need. Let this initial list of prospects supply further names of others who might be interested in a new class dedicated to addressing the need, and then invite these people to come to the organizational meeting.

The initial leadership core for the new class will probably be present at this organizational meeting. This leadership core will not be elected, but will be self-selected: If a person wants to do the job, that person gets it. Each leader commits to being in class and doing a task for six months. At the end of that time, the class can decide what officers are needed and how to choose the officers. But any new class needs continuity to get started. Six months of commitment for specific tasks by specific people helps create that continuity. When six to eight people are willing to fill the leadership needs listed above, you have enough commitment to start a new class.

No church can simply create a class. New classes need consistency and vision. Unless they develop this from within the class members themselves, the class will never become viable. If you cannot find eight people willing to commit to attending a class and to performing leadership functions, then you probably have not located a really significant need. The energy for the class has to come from within, and this energy must be present from the beginning.

At times, the nucleus groups will wrestle with the fact that they took these leadership positions on themselves. Many people naturally feel that they ought not to proclaim themselves president or leader. No one wants to look undemocratic or even arrogant. When faced with these impulses stress the following:

1. In six months the class will have the right to decide its own structure and elect whomever it wishes.
2. They are serving in order to get the class started. Classes need six months to sort out who is really interested in the class and who is not. Anything less means excluding people too soon, or making people commit before they are ready to serve.
3. Every task you do must be done well—especially during the first few weeks. Therefore, choosing leaders from those who want to do the task makes sense—these are the people most likely to do it well.

Sometimes, churches try to begin classes through the use of a sponsor who does not really fit into the relational pattern of the class, but who brings maturity and stability to the class. For example, a singles class might have an older couple who mentor the class and provide stability and consistency. However, such classes rarely work well. When the leadership of the class comes from outside, the people in the class never feel a sense of ownership and responsibility. Newcomers are not attracted because they sense little vision and energy in the class coming from their peers.

When people come to an adult class, they want to find a group that addresses their needs. A visitor should look at the class and say, "Here are people I find interesting and friendly." Leaders from outside the group itself do not lend that point of identification.

Leadership Is the Key

Once you have gathered together a core group of people willing to commit themselves to six months of leadership, you need to make sure that you get the right leaders for the right tasks. Although you want the leaders to volunteer for the tasks, be fair to your volunteers. Outline the essential tasks that need to be done and the skills required. Leadership determines the health of new classes—indeed, all Sunday school classes. Classes need leadership that in general:

* is inclusive and inviting
* gives a sense of purpose and definition
* provides continuity and stability
* provides welcome and caring
* creates excitement and order in the class

Plus, certain tasks must be done. Describing the nature of each leadership task and the qualities needed for each helps the nucleus group make good decisions. Each task is important, and each requires different abilities. This is a team project in which each person provides his or her best skill.

Each leadership team must cover the following critical tasks:

Upfront leadership. Someone has to stand up and direct the flow of the class so that the class is organized and focused. The best upfront leaders are friendly, inviting, work well with groups, and are above all *interested.* People coming into a new class look to the public leaders to define the class. If they see someone who is positive and engaging, they are more likely to stay. Most people also connect good organization with purpose, stability, and security. If the persons leading the class reflect this, more people will stay.

This does not mean that the upfront leader must be highly charismatic or dominating. They simply need to be comfortable with themselves and able to take charge and lead the action of the class. The nucleus group may decide the actual structure of the class, and the upfront leader may simply carry this out, but someone has to lead the actual class session. Finding a person who enjoys leading groups and who creates a good atmosphere in the class will greatly help the development of the class.

Greet and welcome people. The toughest task in the world for most adults is walking into a new group of people. New social groups create fear. Most folks fear that no one will talk to them. They fear not saying the right thing. They fear having to learn new names. They fear rejection! Anyone who remembers their first day at a new school or new job remembers the added stress a new group means for people. The new class leadership should try to create an atmosphere that makes the process as comfortable as possible.

The best solution is to appoint a person or persons who welcome everyone who comes through the door and introduce them to someone else. This seems simple, but unless someone has the responsibility for the task, you may find everyone waiting for someone else to make the first move.

I once read that the number one fear of most people was speaking in public before strangers. Yet, what do most Sunday school classes do? They have visitors stand up and introduce themselves! People feel much better being introduced than introducing themselves. Greeters should, therefore, get someone in the class to meet and then introduce visitors.

The welcoming leaders may also be assigned hospitality tasks like preparing coffee and name tags. Coffee and name tags provide critical opportunities for fellowship. Eating and drinking together has always been a time for socializing in our society. Just having coffee gives people all sorts of opportunities for small talk and beginning social exchanges. Name tags eliminate the problem of not remembering names. People naturally avoid embarrassment. If we do not know someone's name, our tendency is to avoid talking with them in order to hide our ignorance. This means newcomers are excluded.

Often, the persons who take up the greeting function go on to develop a list of new and prospective members and some means of communicating with people outside the class hour. A telephone directory may be printed or a telephone chain created for passing along information. This is important. The more communication going on in a new class, the more likely the class will survive.

Plan social events. Classes grow more quickly if they have some structure for developing the social relationships begun at the class hour. Most often this takes place through social events—supper, times for games, retreats, and so on. Again, the sooner the people in the class have an opportunity to meet one another outside the class hour, the stronger the relational bond will be.[1] Leaders organize and plan these events.

Small, subgroup meetings also perform a socializing function. These may be formed as fixed membership groups, changing membership groups, or some combination. The small subgroups may meet for prayer, Bible study, or some other type of study. The study is useful, but the opportunity to get to know people and develop relationships provides the more powerful motivation for small groups in classes.

Provide emotional support and care. My wife asked, "Are you putting something in the book about the importance of the caring the class does for its members?" She is right. One of the actions that will bring a class together is organizing to care for one another.

A friend gave me an example from his church. A young family experienced a grave illness. Their son contacted spinal meningitis and had to be hospitalized thirty miles from their home. Their class immediately organized to offer support and practical assistance—food, baby-sitting, and running errands. For the young family, this became the event that bonded them to the church, but that event also cemented the class together. Reaching out to help one of their own made the class a unified community.

Classes develop unity and relationships as they care for one another. This caring includes making sure that help is offered at times of illness or hospitalization, sending cards when a loved one dies, and helping the needs and hurts of individuals in the class. Again, this is more likely to happen if someone has the responsibility to make it happen. Ideally, you want a tactful, empathetic, but organized person to do this. Initially, in a new class this position may be part of the welcoming/greeting responsibility or the social responsibility. But the sooner the class members begin caring for one another, the sooner the class will develop a sense of identity and unity.

Plan mission and outreach projects. While the social, relational needs of the class often dominate the early organization of the class, most classes benefit from an early emphasis on service. If the adult class is to help us develop as Christians and individuals, it must encourage us to serve.

Adult classes thrive and grow in service. Traditional activities like putting together Thanksgiving baskets as well as exotic events such as a trip to a foreign setting invigorate and encourage people. The new class does not need extravagant projects. But the class leadership will find that planning some form of ministry will give meaning and depth to the class and draw members together.

Plan and lead music and worship for the class. Music is one of the few activities groups really do together. Most class time is spent with a few people speaking or doing, while the rest watch, receive, or listen. But all sing together. Music can unify a group and build emotional bonds.

Adult classes, especially younger classes, enjoy music. For older classes the typical pattern is to take the hymnal (perhaps a hymnal different from the one used in the sanctuary, with more gospel hymns) and sing along with the piano. For younger classes, you may have someone lead with a guitar and follow a chorus on an overhead, but to do this you must have someone who can lead music. They must feel comfortable singing in front of a group. They must be able to play some instrument reasonably well. They need to know where to find songs that most people already know and can sing. And they must know how to pace the music time.

Music badly done is worse than no music. If the music is too slow, or if no one knows the songs, the result can be more irritating than helpful. Your goal is to sing two songs (four at most) that focus the class and provide a sense of unity and worship. The music leaders need to be prepared. Younger classes like to move smoothly and quickly from one song to the next. Delays and uncertainty feel uncomfortable and uninviting to newcomers.

If you can find a competent and sensitive music leader for a new class, you have something great to build upon. Without the right music leader, the class will do better to concentrate on greeting and incorporating people.

What about teachers? Teachers do not have to be part of the group itself. Most classes appreciate teaching that offers a viewpoint outside their own and expertise in addition to their own. *As long as the teacher does not run the class, the teacher can be an outside source that comes into the class to facilitate the educational function of the class.* The class leaders lead the class, develop the format of the class, and plan the social and ministry functions of the class. The teacher comes into the class to provide information and guidance in learning.

The church can help the new class by providing curriculum and teaching that meet the perceived needs of the class. One church developed a specific set of topics especially for newlyweds covering communication, sex, conflict resolution, relationships with in-laws, developing career and family goals, and the like. The course took about six months to complete. The fact that the church took responsibility for the teaching and content function of the class helped the leadership of the newlywed class to concentrate on the relational function.

New classes that try to do both the relational and the teaching functions often struggle. Since most of the members are new in the church, the leaders are not familiar with the resources available and do not find the right material or instructors. The leadership core spends too much time just finding a teacher and too little time in forming relationships. Separating the teaching function from class leadership helps concentrate the energies of new classes on the primary task of forming relationships and integrating new people.

Getting Started

Once the leadership nucleus is formed, the leadership assignments accepted, the teacher located, and the curriculum agreed upon, you are ready to start the class. Next comes fixing the location of the class. Ideally, the room will be easy to find, nicely furnished, and clean. The room and the leadership together influence the first impression people form of the class. New classes depend on good first impressions more than most. They need positive, accessible space. Too often, churches assign the worst, smallest, least desirable room to new classes. Inferior space creates a barrier for new people—just the people the church is trying to win. At all costs, avoid sending the people around convoluted hallways searching for the room—some will give up the search! A decent room in an easy-to-find location goes a long way toward getting a class off to a good start.

Next, the class needs to find people. Most people come to classes where someone has personally invited them to visit. The leadership nucleus should make lists of their friends and invite them. Advertising the new class in the church newspaper or announcement time in the service will also help. These messages should announce the formation of the class several weeks before you start, and again several weeks after the class has been started (probably six to ten announcements are needed). The people acting as greeters for the church have to be given written descriptions of the class and its purpose (and location).

Buy a coffeepot for the class so that from the beginning they have a focal point for socializing. The first class meeting should focus on welcoming people, helping them to get to know one another, and explaining the purpose of the class. Some nonthreatening, icebreaker questions can be used in these introductions.[2] The purpose of the first meeting is to set the tone for the class and develop relationships. The first "lesson" does little more than outline the goals for the teaching in the weeks ahead and introduce the teacher. The real point is both to state the purpose of the class and to demonstrate this through the structure of the class time.

Set a goal for thirty minutes of teaching and forty minutes of fellowship in your adult classes. Some classes will want more time for teaching, but this is their decision. New classes need to spend even more time on relationship building than established classes, so structure the teaching accordingly—either teach less or incorporate relationship building into the teaching.

The goal of the first class session is *not* to establish a membership list. People are not asked to join the class immediately, but are given a taste of the nature of the class and invited back. A formal membership list might not be set for some months. Keep track of those who come, in order to communicate with them.

Within a few weeks, classes usually want a list of attenders with phone numbers so they can call one another. Within the first couple of weeks, you will want to have a class social, preferably away from the church. The first class "ministry" will probably take place after two or three months, but before the end of the six-month commitment of the nucleus team. During this time, the class continues to advertise its start in the church paper.

Embrace Differences

One of the opportunities in starting new classes is the chance to include people who are on the fringe of your church. One of the classes we did not start at a church I served, but should have, was a class for young, married, noncollege couples. We had these couples in the church (for a while), but they did not find their way into our newlywed classes (who tended toward older and more professional-type members). Because we had no group for them to join, many drifted away over time unless some other, normally family, relationship kept them at church. Looking back, we see that we missed an opportunity.

Many special groups can find a place in a church if someone finds them and makes them welcome. Earlier, I mentioned parents of special needs children. Too often they find it difficult to connect with churches because so few in a particular church share their needs. Single parents are another group (and a growing group) that find they do not quite fit in a regular married couples class or a singles class. A class does not have to be large to be successful, if *successful* means helping a group of people. Adult classes can be a means of increasing the overall diversity of the church and reaching out to new types of people if we look for them.

Start Classes, Do Not Split Them

Classes do not split well. Classes are networks of friendships and relationships. These networks are never simple. Splitting classes inevitably causes problems, because you can never get all the right friends in one class.

First United Methodist Tulsa in the 1970s went to two parallel church services and adult class hours (9:30 A.M. and

10:50 A.M.). The attempt was made to take some of the larger classes at 9:30 A.M. and split them into 9:30 A.M. and 10:50 A.M. classes. When I came in 1982 to the church, I could see the results of this attempt. In the end, none of the splits worked. Either a completely new class was formed at 10:50, or one of the two classes essentially failed. For example, the Fellowship Class had been a strong 9:30 class in 1976, averaging around fifty persons a week. In the 1980s the Fellowship class was struggling somewhat and averaging about half that number. Many of the original class members had left the church. The 10:50 version of the class (the Friendship Class) was doing well, but was filled almost entirely with new members.

The 10:50 hour of classes finally worked, but most of the strong classes came through forming new classes, not through splits. Over time, a number of newlywed classes started at 10:50, several growing to average fifty or more persons per Sunday. Even some strong classes for older couples were started, but not through splits.

I believe that splitting classes is usually too difficult and too painful to work as a means of starting new classes. You can work with class *dropouts* and try to form a new class from people who have not found their place in an existing class. If their reasons for dropping out are purely negative, however, dropouts are not fertile ground for new classes. But if they represent some positive but unmet needs, you can build on these.

Whatever the background or circumstances, remember:

Find a need
Gather a committed leadership nucleus.
Develop a structure to meet the need.
Provide the teaching.
Contact your potential members.
Start with an emphasis on developing relationships.

These are basic building blocks for starting new classes.

V

RECRUITING TEACHERS IS EASIER THAN TRAINING THEM

Someone asked a certain college football coach, "How did you become such a good coach?" He answered quickly, "I don't coach players, I recruit them."

The concept applies to adult learning: recruiting good teachers is easier than training them. Several times our church attempted courses which sought to make willing volunteers into teachers. The results were not encouraging. People came to the classes and did their assignments faithfully, but few grew into really effective teachers. On the other hand the people we found who already had teaching and communication skills could easily take good material and succeed as teachers.

This is not to say that people cannot learn to become more effective communicators. I recently attended a professional seminar on communication. We all began by giving a short talk that was videotaped. Generally, we looked awful. Three days later, after much work and thinking about communication, we were taped again. We all looked and communicated much better! But rarely can church leaders spend this amount of time with their teachers, and few churches can afford expert communications instructors to train their people. Moreover, even though every member of our seminar improved, I am not sure how many of us would function well as public speakers on a regular basis.

Not Everyone Can Teach

Why are some gifted teachers while some are not? No definitive answer exists. That is like asking why some college professors are extremely knowledgeable in their area with years of lecturing experience, and yet still fail as teachers. Some great scholars teach effectively. Some do not.

New Testament lists of the gifts of the Holy Spirit give teaching major status (1 Cor. 12:28; Eph. 4:11). The variety of the gifts, according to Paul, means that no one possesses all the gifts, nor is there one gift that all possess. Instead, people receive different gifts for different ministries. Paul encourages the church to celebrate the gift of every person and let each person minister according to his or her gifts. This means that some people will be good at teaching, while others may struggle to be merely adequate. Wise leaders try to find people who thrive by teaching and let them teach.

Churches often approach teaching primarily in terms of content. If a person knows a great deal about a subject, then we invite him or her to teach. However, having knowledge or even experience is not the same as being able to teach others. One church naturally went to experienced counselors for a particular course on personal development. These counselors developed the material and taught the course, along with some regular Sunday school teachers who were not counselors. The regular teachers took the material, and though it was new to them, they did well. The experienced counselors knew the material extremely well, but they struggled trying to teach it. Assuming that having gifts in one area translates into an ability to teach about that area proved to be mistaken.

The Importance of Not Just Filling Slots

Churches err when they ask the wrong people to teach, and they err again when they ask the right persons, but fail to support them. The pressure to have a warm body in front of every class becomes the primary concern in some churches, which then sometimes fail to follow through to make sure the teachers they find succeed.

A university professor shared his own frustrating experience. A fine teacher in his field, he was asked by his church to teach an adult Bible study class. With some hesitation he said yes, and the leaders thrust a load of material in his arms and disappeared.

The professor was a successful teacher, but not a Bible scholar. The course was open-ended and ill-defined in terms of his commitment. He had no one to call on as a substitute when he traveled. He studied his material but received little formal feedback. As a proud and dedicated teacher, it was a frustrating experience. He finally quit and has never taught since.

This professor had real potential as a teacher of an adult class. In the haste to fill slots, the leaders forever ruined him for teaching in the church. Many teachers encounter a similar experience. Asked to do too big of a job, and given too little support, they end up frustrated. Churches need to recruit people who are good at teaching and help these people become successful. Every success makes future recruiting easier. Every frustrated teacher makes future recruiting harder. If church people view teaching as a rewarding and fulfilling experience, recruiting becomes a much easier task. The challenge is to create the sense that what we are asking people to do, they can do.

Create Doable Tasks

Recruiting good teachers requires defining the task of teaching so that people feel they can reasonably do the job. Four tools can make teaching look much more doable:

1. Limit the term of commitment.
2. Limit the number of lessons.
3. Provide for time off and substitutes.
4. Provide good teaching material.

Each of these tools helps to answer fears and concerns that many people have when they are asked to teach.

First, limiting the term of commitment makes teaching much easier to contemplate. Give every teacher a start date and a stop date. The longest term of commitment should be a year. At the end of the year, you should have the right to ask them to teach again, or not. Even more important, the teacher should have the right not to teach again if she or he wants to quit. If teachers choose to quit, avoid the temptation to make them feel guilty for putting the church in a bind. If you recruit by guilt, people will learn to avoid you now so that they can miss the guilt later. When people know that they are committing to a definite term of teaching and will be completely free to continue or not if asked, they can say yes more easily. Long-term commitments are anathema to many baby boomers, so limited-term commitments are especially necessary to reach them, and a courtesy to everyone else.[1]

Second, limit the number of lessons a teacher has to teach. Each year contains fifty-two Sundays. Being asked to teach a new lesson (even from a quarterly) every Sunday is a Herculean task. Unless people have the time or love research, coming up with new lessons every week can overwhelm them.

This may sound like it would increase your recruiting problem by multiplying the number of teachers you need. A solution: Ask teachers to teach the same course more than once in different classes. Instead of having six teachers in six classes teaching forty-eight lessons each (assuming four weeks off for good behavior), why not have six teachers prepare eight lessons, and teach these lessons several times in different classes? Instead of preparing new lessons every week, the teacher can simply take the material prepared and share it with a new audience.

We found that rotating teachers and courses made the prospect of teaching much more plausible to many people. We were able to recruit teachers and tell them that they would be responsible for teaching eight lessons on a given topic or Bible book. They would teach those same lessons three or four times in a twelve-month period. We cut preparation time drastically and made the burden lighter. Teaching the material more than once also gave most teachers increased confidence in their teaching. Most found that teaching a course the second or third time allowed them to add to their material and polish their presentation. They did not teach the course enough to get stale in their teaching, but they had a chance really to master a subject.

The main objection to this process is the fact that many, if not most, adult classes have traditionally had one teacher who was "their" teacher. How do you get the class to share the teacher, and the teacher to leave "his" or "her" class?

Some people will not want to change. But this process offers major benefits for teacher and class:

* If teachers have fewer lessons to prepare, they are usually better prepared. The rotation process will normally improve teaching by making the preparation more focused.
* If teachers rotate, all the classes get a change of pace. Variety is fun both for teachers and classes.
* If teachers rotate, classes share the best teachers instead of possessing just one. The whole church gets stronger instead of just one or two special classes.
* If teachers rotate, the teachers get to present their work to a wider variety of people. Many teachers enjoy getting to know and influence a broader section of people in the church.
* If teachers rotate, the recruitment of more and better teachers becomes easier. This helps every class and relieves classes of the burden of "filling the slot" every Sunday.

Even this explanation will not be enough to convince everyone. But if you can convince one or two classes to try this, and perhaps start a new class and include them in the rotation, the results will influence those who hold back.

Third, you create doable tasks if you build into the teaching schedule both times off for the teacher and easy-to-find substitutes. You can do this through the creation of *teacher teams*. Each teacher is a part of a team of teachers who teach the same course. This does not mean the team teaches the course in the same class together. Rather, each teacher presents the course individually in a particular class. The team concept comes to play in the way you develop courses, assign teachers, and provide substitutes.

The process works something like this: Develop an outline for each course. Then, recruit a team of teachers for the course. Team members then agree to the following:

A. Each teacher will teach three or four, two-month periods during the year. Ideally, each will teach for two months and then be off for two months.
B. When not teaching, each teacher will be available to substitute for those teaching. This means if you need to be gone a week during your two-month teaching time, you know who is available to call as a substitute, and that these people are familiar with your lessons. The team members help one another with their scheduling needs. If you have to substitute and do not get your full two months off, at least you know that others will help you out, too.

The team prepares lessons and discusses material together. As you begin your curriculum each year, the teams of teachers meet to discuss the outline prepared for the course and to add their own thoughts and ideas. During the first few months of the curriculum, the teams meet again and discuss how the course is going—what is working and what is not. The teachers provide resources for one another in terms of methods and materials. If one develops a handout, he or she shares with the others. If one finds a good book to read, he or she shares it with the other teachers. The team concept multiplies the benefits of the work of all.

Teaching becomes doable when teachers have helpful teaching material. Knowing that you will give them good material and support in teaching helps teachers want to teach.

Different ways of developing curriculum is a matter for our next chapter. The point for now is that confidence in your curriculum resources makes recruitment easier.

Allow for Creativity

People volunteer for any service for two reasons: They believe they can succeed in the task, and they believe the service offers an opportunity for personal expression. Recent studies show that even on the job, younger workers want more than money and advancement. Many workers express, "a keen desire to understand the total picture in the workplace . . . they are not content simply to follow orders."[2] If this is true for workers, how much more does the sense of accomplishing something meaningful motivate our volunteers?[3]

When we developed curriculum, we wanted to cover certain areas of content. But we insisted that teachers teach the material in a way that suited them. Naturally, if the course was supposed to cover the Gospel of Luke, we expected them to teach Luke, not the book of Revelation. But we did not insist on a rigid adherence to the outline. We knew that many would go about the teaching task in a different way, with a different emphasis. Some teachers lecture. Some teachers use discussion. If you are a good lecturer, by all means lecture![4] Letting teachers find their own style of teaching was much more helpful than trying to standardize a particular format.

If teachers can choose their style of teaching and make the class personable and a reflection of themselves, then they will enjoy teaching. Having them stick too closely to a curriculum or style can make recruiting much harder. Some good teachers, of course, are happy to follow the outline closely, But all need the freedom to put their own creative energy into the course.

Evaluate Teachers

Recruiting teachers becomes easier if they know you expect excellence. This may sound contradictory. Will not high expectations scare people off? If people do not think they can meet the expectations, they may be scared off. But if we have high expectations of our teachers, our recruitment of them becomes a compliment. We are thereby suggesting that we see them as excellent teachers. Teaching in an adult class becomes an honor when people know that expectations are high.

Near the end of each two-month course, the education staff person or Sunday school superintendent can send each class president or leader an evaluation form. The form will allow the class leader to rate the teacher and the course in terms of interest, content, delivery, class involvement, and topic.

Most comments will be very positive, but the evaluations help those responsible for adult education curriculum in the church spot potential trouble areas. If the course content is too abstract, or the teacher too preachy, the class leaders will have the opportunity to make their opinions known. Sometimes, the personality of the teacher and class may not mix well. In either case, the evaluations will help churches see how to help individual teachers do a better job.

You may be wary of sharing negative evaluations with teachers. I did not share evaluations directly, in order to avoid problems with individual teachers and classes. However, I did share the general feedback with the teachers. Most of the time the feedback was positive, and the negatives could be shared by simply framing the information in a positive way. If a class suggested that a teacher was failing to allow for class discussion, I would go to the teacher and say something like this, "Here's what I think would make you a better teacher: ask at least four or five questions for discussion each lesson, and make sure the people have a chance to interact with what you are saying." Helpful feedback does not have to be threatening.

Alternatively, the pastor or Sunday school superintendent could share a summary report of evaluations with teachers. These reports could highlight both strengths and areas for improvement. Most teachers appreciate knowing how classes assessed their work—the positives and the negatives.[5] Expecting teachers to work carefully on their teaching will raise the standards of instruction in your classes.

What Does a Good Teacher Look Like?

You can recruit good teachers when you create a climate where people believe that they can succeed in teaching. But how do you know whom to recruit? Adult educators list the following as characteristics people appreciate in teachers:

* knowledgeable in their subject
* relate theory to practice
* appear confident
* open to different approaches
* present an authentic personality to the class
* create a good atmosphere for learning
* courteous
* good humored
* tactful
* energetic
* articulate
* imaginative
* use learners' experiences[6]

In an informal and unscientific survey of pastors, two qualities were found in most effective teachers: character and the ability to communicate. Good teachers find a way to connect with people, and they make connection through both who they are and what they say.

Sometimes good teachers are especially outgoing and enthusiastic, and sometimes they are not. But good teachers always have a way of making their listeners feel important and valued, of entering into the world of the class, and of making the material personal and relevant.

Communication skills, however, are only part of the story. The characters of the teachers must match what they teach. People listen most to mature persons with integrity. This means that when people were going through personal problems, for their own sake and the sake of the classes, they need not to teach. Therefore, when you look for good teachers, you try to find people who are respected for their life-style and faith, and who communicate well. Bible knowledge helps, and classes appreciate those who understand good teaching methods and discussion techniques. But the real keys are character and the ability to connect with people and make faith relevant.[7]

One pastor describing his favorite teacher said, "Most people, just looking at him, would never 'peg' him as any kind of leader." No simple teacher "type" exists. So how do you find them? Generally, the best indicator of future success is past success. The good communicators in your church will already be communicating somewhere. One way to find them is to look to fields that demand good communication: teachers, lawyers, salesmen, and the like. Naturally, not every professional teacher or lawyer makes a good teacher (some teachers want a break from teaching when they attend church!). But, in general, those who are already successful in "people" professions have gathered communication and relational skills that can make them good teachers of adults.

Be open, however, to people who are not in these obvious professions. Ask members of the class, "Who do you think would make a good teacher in your class? Who is good at communicating in a group?" Every once in a while, this sort of questioning turns up a name not previously considered.

A director of Christian education told of a great teacher she found in this way. He sold computers professionally. Computer types are not always good with people, but she decided to follow up on the suggestion. She contacted him, and he was interested in the idea of teaching. The two arranged an interview and then she gave him an assignment with another teacher. He quickly became one of their very best. Asking for suggestions and then following up to meet with and talk with these people gave this church significant new recruitment possibilities.

Note how the church developed this teacher. Once the staff person recruited the computer salesman, she wanted to break him into teaching slowly. For people with little background in teaching, many churches set up an apprenticeship with an experienced teacher. The new teacher attends and listens to one course, discussing with the mentoring teacher his or her method of teaching. Then, the two teachers alternate teaching one course for a period (the mentor one Sunday, the new teacher the next). Finally, the new teacher teaches for a period,

with the mentoring teacher observing and offering suggestions and encouragement. The mentor provides a model for
the new teacher, and a chance to break into the teaching
experience slowly.

Okay, You Do Some Training, Too

Obviously, what we described above falls under the category of training. An emphasis on recruiting gifted teachers
does not exclude training. But remember that while training
supports teachers, training rarely supplies teachers.

In addition to the team meetings and the apprenticeship
period, teachers of adults appreciate other types of training.
Occasional presentations by educational experts help. Most
school systems now have people who are trained in adult
education and who can speak meaningfully to a church on the
particular needs of adults. They can present material on how
to lead class discussions and how to teach more concisely.
Content and methodology training does help teachers.[8]

Perhaps the best training comes in peer-learning sessions.
Simply invite the larger group of teachers to get together and
share whatever is going well in their teaching. Let someone
present a problem and have the whole group offer solutions.
Because the teachers all teach in the same church and the same
classes, they will understand the situation better than most
outside professionals and will offer one another practical and
relevant insights.

These training sessions not only provide knowledge; they
also promote community, creating a bond among teachers and
a sense of shared mission. Teachers will become friends and
co-workers. The training session may do more for *esprit de corps*
than anything else. A sense of mission and accomplishment
among teachers at a church also makes recruiting easier next
year. Getting the right people in the first place makes adult
learning in the church effective. Helping the teachers feel
positive about their experience keeps adult learning effective
for the long haul.

VI

CUSTOM-FIT CURRICULUM

The Circle Class was founded in 1929. Most of the Circle Class are long-time members. They are all retired, many widowed. They are traditionalists for the most part. Their favorite teacher is older, with a preachy style. You can set your watch by the way they run their class: opening at 9:30 A.M., followed by two hymns, a devotional, the care report, prayer, birthdays and anniversaries, the offering, and the lesson.

The Koinonia Class is a singles class. Almost all the members are under thirty years old, have never been married, and are in their first full-time job. Few have grown up in the denomination. The class changes format frequently. They sing choruses and use a guitar. New people come all the time. Generally, people leave as they either marry or move due to job demands.

Imagine teaching both classes! Is there one course that could possibly fit both? How could one find or develop curriculum to fit the needs of both classes? Forming curriculum that will stretch to meet the needs of classes as different as the Circle Class and the Koinonia class is possible, but demands good planning and flexible teachers.

71

Developing Overall Goals for Your Adult Education

Curriculum needs a direction. The concerns of people will provide shape for that direction, but some overall goals that give your program coherence and long-term direction will make the courses more relevant, not less.

In general, each curriculum explores the following:

* Biblical study (study from both testaments, Old and New)
* Theological issues (study of the basic doctrines of faith)
* Practical applications of faith

Here are some reasonable five-year goals for a balanced curriculum:

1. *Study the entire New Testament over a five-year period.* This does not mean a verse-by-verse study of each book. Rather, the goal anticipates some study from each book of the New Testament in lessons over this period. Brief surveys or thematic studies fit the Sunday morning format best. Most classes want Bible study, but many classes will have a mix of people in terms of their background and interest in Bible study. A course that can offer both introduction to the newcomer and some opportunity for reflection and discussion for the long-time participant will probably serve most classes well. Sunday morning serves the need for more basic Bible study, with the emphasis on application to life. More advanced Bible study will fit in at other times.

2. *Introduce the five major areas of the Old Testament (Pentateuch, Histories, Major Prophets, Minor Prophets, Wisdom Literature).* In our surveys, Old Testament courses always came out among the least desired offerings. Nevertheless, in order to understand the New Testament and our Jewish heritage, some study of the Old Testament is needed. The five major sections of the Old Testament cover the basic history and types of literature of ancient Judaism. Over a period of years, these courses introduce people to the Old Testament. The Sunday morning courses serve more to help reduce the strangeness of the

Old Testament to our classes than anything else. Other formats offer opportunities for more advanced studies. Lively teachers with the ability to make material clear and personal are most helpful in Old Testament courses. Classes often value these courses more highly after they take them.

3. *Deal with one or more significant theological themes or issues.* People do wrestle with basic theological issues—such as the nature of faith, grace, Christology, and the like. These courses, however, connect with the interest of the classes rather than follow some arbitrary scheme. When people were reacting strongly to the TV evangelist scandals, classroom surveys revealed questions about the nature of faith and the possibility of healing. The high point of the charismatic renewal spawned several courses on the Holy Spirit. Tracking what is covered year to year helps to balance out the overall course offerings, but the most successful theological courses will tie into the questions people are asking.

4. *Offer one or more courses related to the practical application of the faith.* People ask all the time, "How should I pray?" "What does a Christian really need to do with money?" These and other such questions reflect a desire to apply one's faith to the reality of life in work, family, and with oneself. Certain topics (such as family, finances, and missions) demand periodic treatment. Other topics may arise through surveys of class members. Here, above all, the expressed needs of the class provide the best guide to the most important topics to cover.

Therefore, the first step in custom fitting a curriculum is to survey the needs of your classes. You can begin with an informal survey, simply paying attention to what people are doing. Keeping your ears open and listening to what people are discussing will provide a good bit of informal guidance. What are people reading? What are they talking about? What questions do they ask one another and their pastor?

The ideas you gather from this informal process will help you to structure a more formal survey of the adult classes. Well before you anticipate beginning a new curriculum, send a survey questionnaire out to each class president (or class leader). The survey can guide the president in conferring with others in the class so that his or her answers represent a consensus of the class.

The survey allows members of each class an opportunity to rank their interest in a range of topics, and to provide input into the selection of courses for the coming year. The following would represent a short-form of this type of survey.

Rate the following as areas of interest for your class ("1" being lowest, "5" being the highest interest):
_____ Prayer
_____ Social justice
_____ Parenting
_____ Couples Communication
_____ Racial injustice
_____ Handling financial stress
_____ Other (please write in ideas)

The topics represent what seems to be the interests of the classes based on your informal knowledge. A good survey provides choice, but too many choices may make the rankings meaningless. Something around ten to fifteen topic selections will give the classes a good range of ideas to consider. The questionnaire also includes some space for the classes to add their own concerns.

The results of the survey go to a group of representatives from the classes. The group allows you to test your understanding of what the surveys were saying. At this point it will become clear where particular needs among the classes differ. Our goal, as described in the previous chapter, was to rotate teachers from class to class with the same course. With good planning we could organize the courses, however, to meet several needs.

For example, our younger classes typically want something that addresses the pressure points of their lives: children, career, finances. The older classes, however, have little or no interest in these things. We might, however, be able to come up with a Christian stewardship course that stressed budgeting and dealing with tight finances to younger classes, but retirement planning with older classes. Much of the core biblical and theological concepts developed for the course would apply to all ages. The difference in the courses would be the application of the material around the interest areas of the individual class. Identifying the needs we wanted to address at the beginning helped us to begin building flexibility into the content design of the courses.

We could never meet all the needs identified with any one curriculum. Meeting with the class representatives helped us to prioritize what needs would be met in a given year's courses. Some ideas would be postponed for later courses, or would be shifted to another means of adult learning. For example a deep concern about family abuse issues might be taken up in a course in our non-Sunday teaching programs instead of being a topic in an adult lesson series.

Consider Two-Month Courses Instead of Three

The outline of curriculum above assumes that each course lasts two months. We tested the question of course length by offering courses of various lengths of time and following the attendance pattern. Interest in courses peaked in the first few weeks, and remained constant until the eighth week, and then began to decline. At the end of two months, people would be saying, "Gee, I wish this would go on longer." But by three months, more and more people were saying, "When will this be over?"

The two-month cycle offers many advantages. First, as we suggested in the last chapter, you put less pressure on your teachers—eight lessons are easier to prepare than twelve or thirteen. Second, the shorter term fits our culture better. People like change and variety. They do not make long-term commitments.

The shorter term also softens mistakes. The teacher will not always mesh well with a class. If people do not like the teacher, they often will stop coming to class. In a two-month course, some who do not respond to a certain teacher will still come for the social function of the class. Those who do not come will be out of the class for a shorter time and will be more likely to start up again when the course changes. Shorter course length minimizes the effect of mistakes.

Several negatives to the two-month courses come to mind. First, this means developing six courses, not four. More courses require more subjects and more teachers. Second, most prepared curriculum follows a three-month pattern. Six courses require searching for alternatives to the standard quarterly, or adapting curriculum, or developing your own curriculum. All of this suggests six courses may demand more time—a precious commodity.

The variety and the flexibility of the two-month courses justifies the effort. Churches that feel that they lack the teacher and time resources to develop two-month courses will want to stick with the three-month schedule. However, even these need to consider how to make three-month courses more relevant and interesting.

Rotating Teachers on a Two-Month Curriculum

Rotating teachers from class to class with a two-month curriculum means that a church needs six courses for a one-year program and a plan for rotating courses and teachers through every class.

Sample Curriculum Schedule

Six Courses:

	Title	Subject (teachers)
#1	First Letters	Bible study of I and II Thessalonians (Jones and Smith)
#2	First Gospel	Bible study of Mark (Brown and Johnson)
#3	First Kings	Bible study of I and II Kings (Lincoln and Douglas)
#4	First Faith	A study of the basics of the Christian faith (Lloyd and Law)
#5	First Fruits	Understanding and applying the fruits of the Spirit to daily life (Long and Ball)
#6	First Principles	Power and authority: how the Christian lives with this reality (May and King)

Rotation Schedule

Class	Sept/Oct	Nov/Dec	Jan/Feb	Mar/Ap	May/Jun	Jul/Au
Builders	#1	#2	#3	#4	#5	#6
	Jones	Johnson	Lincoln	Law	Long	King
Circle	#2	#3	#4	#5	#6	#1
	Brown	Douglas	Lloyd	Ball	May	Smith
Joynors	#3	#4	#5	#6	#1	#2
	Lincoln	Law	Long	King	Jones	Johnson
Friendship	#4	#5	#6	#1	#2	#3
	Lloyd	Ball	May	Smith	Brown	Douglas
Koinonia	#5	#6	#1	#2	#3	#4
	Long	King	Jones	Johnson	Lincoln	Law
One Accord	#6	#1	#2	#3	#4	#5
	May	Smith	Brown	Douglas	Lloyd	Ball

This nice, neat schedule assumes six courses, six adult classes, and twelve teachers (two per course). In this scheme each teacher offers his or her course three times over the year, and has three, two-month periods off. Churches with fewer or more classes or teachers will still want to design a similar rotation schedule for their situation. More than six classes probably means having more than two teachers for each course (because you will need to offer the same course in more than one class at a time). Note that you can change the "two-months-on/two-months-off" sequence. Sometimes, the desire to match a certain teacher with a certain class may be more important than maintaining this simple schedule. These decisions have to be worked out with teachers and classes. Matching teacher, course, and the needs of the class remains the goal.

Choosing Curriculum

Much good curriculum already exists. Denominational publishing houses provide good materials, as do independent publishers. Prepared curriculum has the enormous advantage of doing the work for you. Good curriculum will organize the lessons, provide clear goals and purposes for each lesson, suggest how to structure the lesson, and advise teachers how to develop discussion and application.

Prepared material does have disadvantages. The publishers choose the subject based on general needs, not the needs of your local church. Similarly, prepared curriculum tries to serve an "average" adult class. Your classes will not fit that exact image. Unless you adapt the material to your own classes, the lessons may lack relevance.

Adult classes also have to wrestle with the fact that Americans read less and less. Curriculum that depends upon people reading printed resources prior to the class may create problems in two areas. Teachers trying to lead a class where some members have read the material and some have not may feel frustrated. You lose one group or the other. Similarly, class members who have not read the lesson may receive a not-so-subtle message: "You do not belong here." The use of prepared lessons prompts two important questions:

How do we adapt this material to our class(es)?

How do we use the published material in ways that include people rather than excludes them?

Churches that commit to a two-month format have another problem: most prepared curriculum follows the quarterly (thirteen-week) format. The decision to go to a two-month format will require adapting the material further by squeezing thirteen lessons into eight or nine. This simply means being more concise and trying to cover less (not longer lessons). Fortunately, more and more publishing houses are coming out with material that assumes shorter length courses. Searching for alternative material suitable for two-month periods pays dividends in increased interest.

Developing Your Own Curriculum

Instead of using prepared curriculum, churches can and do develop their own. This does present challenges. Preparing lessons takes time. A particular church may not have people with the expertise to develop their own lessons. Planning ahead to have lessons and teachers ready becomes essential, and hectic schedules make this difficult.

But consider these benefits:

1. the ability to tailor the lessons to local needs and interests
2. teacher participation in the creative process of developing material
3. developing curriculum that anticipates the different personalities and needs of individual classes

Creating your own curriculum can give your program a distinct identity that will invigorate both teachers and classes.

To design a yearly curriculum you begin with the overall goals you have developed for your church (along the lines developed at the beginning of the chapter) and the needs suggested by the survey of your classes. From this you ask the questions: What courses will help us accomplish our goals and speak to the most pressing needs of our people? Are there biblical studies that will address some questions? Is there a theological or practical problem with which to work? You are looking for six broad ideas, biblical books, or topics that meet your various goals. Once you have six separate ideas, you are ready to take these ideas and develop courses.

The next step is to take each individual idea and construct a purpose statement for each course. Ask yourself, "What is the course trying to accomplish?" This can be stated in a brief sentence or two. The purpose statement should outline clearly the content you intend to teach and your motive for the course. Once you define the overall purpose, then divide that purpose into separate parts that can be covered in a given lesson.

These separate parts will typically relate to specific problems or questions, which together define the overall topic of the course.[1] You are seeking to cover the general purpose of the course in eight separate lessons. Each lesson will tackle a particular question or concern which, together with the other seven lessons, works to address the more general purpose of the course.

Given the problem, most educators suggest a three-step process in developing the individual lessons:

* Determine your objectives
* Determine your content
* Determine your methods[2]

All this means is that each lesson, like the course as a whole, should have a particular goal in mind, normally a particular question or problem to study or answer. In developing the lesson you will need to draw together resources from books or the Bible that give you material relevant to the problem. And you will need to decide how you are going to present this material to the class in order to get your ideas across.

To put it another way, developing a curriculum takes at least five steps:

1. Define a need or topic of interest.
2. Develop a purpose or objective for the course as a whole.
3. Develop several questions or problems that make the topic important.
4. List what you know and your sources for this knowledge about each question or topic.
5. Decide on the methods for teaching the material.

For example, a particular problem for today's Christians is the fact that we live in an increasingly secular world. The interweaving of church, school, home, and workplace, which existed for our parents, does not hold for us or our children. The problem is, How do we as Christians live in a world that is increasingly secular and unaware of or uninterested in Christian things?

Divide this problem into eight key topics:

* The historical movement from Christian to secular society (setting up the problem)
* Problems raised by secularization
* Struggles over ethical issues today
* Evidence for secularization of the church
* Questions raised by the advance of science
* Questions raised by human experience
* Questions raised by diverse opinions within the church
* Synthesis: How can Christians witness to a pluralistic world?

For each lesson, gather resources to address the problem being raised. Look for biblical passages that might shed some light. Find a few key books that deal with the issues (in this case, you might consider C. S. Lewis's book, *The Abolition of Man*).

The question remains: *How do you teach the material?* A lecture can raise the problems and provide analysis and answers all within a monologue. A series of good questions can also lead the class into the problem through discussion. For example, in one lesson begin by asking the class the question, "As Christians, how do we decide what is 'right' and 'wrong'?" In another lesson, begin by showing the introduction to a movie in which religious themes and questions are raised, and ask the class, "What is this movie saying about the church and Christians?" Or give an example of a situation (hypothetical or real) and ask the class to respond. In each of these different methods, the principle is the same: Once you know the problem you are approaching and your goal for the lesson, find a question or life example that will illustrate the problem and get the class thinking.

The structure of the lessons follows this pattern:

* Statement of problem through question or example (or both)
* Biblical material relevant to the question
* Other sources relevant to the question
* Development of possible solutions or approaches

This type of process works well in courses that address theological issues or application of faith to life. Such topical courses require someone in the church to do the basic course development, set up the problem and objectives for each lesson, and find the resources for the lesson. This person may be a pastor or a lay volunteer. Each course has to provide a fairly full outline with suggestions for the teaching team regarding how to teach the material (normally three to four pages per lesson). Developing a full course often takes two or three months. Therefore, churches developing their own curriculum will need to begin these assignments three to six months prior to the date of the first class in order to allow time for lesson development and interaction with other teachers.

The whole process of moving from survey to curriculum might suggest a timetable like this:

January	—Mail out survey.
February	—Meet with class presidents; decide on six course ideas.
March	—Assign six course ideas to individuals to develop outlines.
April	—Discuss eight lesson topics with outline developers.
May/June	—Recruit other teachers.
July/August	—Teaching teams meet to discuss and further develop outlines.
September	—Begin new curriculum.

The method for developing the courses on the Bible parallels this format. A two-month cycle does not allow covering a book verse by verse. Bible studies that concentrate on a theme or section of the book succeed well in adult classes.

Fortunately, many tools are available to help the person who is developing a course on a biblical book. *Teaching the Bible to Adults and Youth* by Dick Murray provides excellent help for Bible study and teaching, as does the book by Gordon D. Fee and Douglas Stuart, *How to Read the Bible for All It's Worth*. Before beginning any development of a Bible course for an adult class, these books would be worth reading for guidance in study and practical advice in developing lessons.[3]

Once you have chosen your book and decided upon your approach to the book (whether to study a section or a theme), divide your task into the appropriate number of lessons. Books tend to fall into discrete sections: episodes, groups of stories or events, or stages in the development of an argument. In Matthew 5–7, for example, we find a section containing the teaching material of Jesus. Within that section, the material is divided into identifiable groups of material: the Beatitudes (Matt. 5:1-11); metaphors for discipleship (5:12-16); teaching about the law (5:17-20); teaching about anger (5:21-26); and so on. A good Bible translation will often give headings to paragraphs or sections as a guide. Use these natural transitions in the text to help organize the material.

Questions draw the class into the content and meaning of the Bible better than anything. Asking good questions takes work, but all questions tend to fall into three types.

Observation questions. These questions help the class to see what is in the text. They ask who, what, where, and when. Observation questions lead the class to see what is going on in the text. The teacher asks the class, "What type of text do we have here?" "Who is involved?" "What happens?" The class can read the text and respond to what they read.

Interpretive questions. After the class has sufficiently noted the surface "facts" of the text, they are ready to move on to meaning. Here, you can ask the class to define important terms. For example, a lesson on the Beatitudes would need to ask, "What does the term *Blessed* mean?" Interpretation also means asking about the significance and implication of acts or images in the text. Again, in studying Matthew 5:13-16, ask the question, "What is the significance of the images of light and salt for this passage?" Interpretive questions define terms and ask about the significance and function of images, actions, and characters in a passage.[4]

Application questions. After defining what the passage is trying to say, the question remains, "What is the passage saying *to us*?" Application questions seek to take the passage and its message and make connections between the world of the passage and the world of the adult class. The teacher may want to link the passage to a particular problem, asking, "What would this idea suggest about the problem raised in the newspaper this week?" Or, "What does this suggest about the way we handle our money?" Application questions try to make concrete connections between the interpretation of the passage and the lives of the people in the class.

The outline of the lesson develops all three types of questions (observation, interpretation, and application) for the passage under study and provides possible answers to guide the teacher. In a lecture format, the teacher raises the questions and then answers them. In a discussion format, the teacher raises the questions and then invites the class to participate in answering. The material from the outline and the study of the teacher then supplement and guide the discussion. Using the question and discussion method of teaching requires some tact. You do not want to ask any questions that the class cannot reasonably answer from reading the text. Questions that assume special background knowledge (due to some special social custom of the ancient world) simply frustrate people. Put the background information on the board or in a handout for people to read. Ask only those questions class members might be expected to know through reading the passage or general knowledge. Otherwise, people will not answer for fear of looking ignorant.

Good discussion also depends on asking questions that generate conversation. Questions that are too obvious kill discussion. Questions that have only one possible answer make discussion boring. And questions that only the teacher can answer obviously do not invite the class to participate.

The best questions offer a chance for the class to have input and the possibility of a variety of answers. Check and see if your questions are sufficiently open-ended—that is, can a person give a variety of answers and still in some sense contribute to the discussion? If the answer is too specific, the class will sense that they are trying to guess what the teacher wants them to say, rather than really thinking and responding to the passage. Again, this kills discussion.

Evaluation

Every curriculum, whoever develops it, benefits from some evaluation. Both teachers and classes should have input into this evaluation. If you have teaching teams, then the teams need to continue meeting past the beginning of the curriculum in order to share with one another the results of teaching. Similarly, survey the classes themselves for their response to the material. The evaluation survey seeks several types of information. Did the lessons actually achieve the purpose and goals of the course? Was the material relevant? Was it presented in a fashion that involved the class and kept interest? Was the information clearly presented?

One effective form of evaluation is simply to send a teacher and course evaluation to every class after the course ends. The president or other class leader can fill these out. Evaluations can use multiple-choice forms to make it easier for the classes to respond. One or two open-ended questions in the evaluation will let the class leader summarize the effectiveness of the course in his or her own words. For example, ask, "Describe in your own words what you liked and didn't like about this course. About this teacher." The forms are then returned to the curriculum leader. Evaluations only help when you use the information you receive. If a particular lesson is not working, change it. If a particular teacher works well in one class, use him or her there again and try to figure out what made him or her successful. If you are rotating curriculum, you create an incentive to improve courses as you go along. But even if you are not rotating courses, evaluation can help you pick better curriculum and better teachers.

Content counts. Lessons that interest people, speak to their needs, and deal with significant issues are fun to teach and fun to hear. Good lessons mean finding good material or writing your own. Either takes work and effort. But if you initiate an evaluation system, you'll find out classes appreciate good content.

Sample Teacher/Curriculum Evaluation

Class: _____

Teacher: _____

Course Title: _____

(Circle one)
    I. The teacher's preparation for class
      1. Consistently prepared
      2. Usually prepared
      3. Sometimes prepared
      4. Seldom prepared
      5. Unprepared

II. Teacher's interest and enthusiasm in subject
   1. Consistently enthusiastic and interested
   2. Frequently enthusiastic and interested
   3. Sometimes enthusiastic and interested
   4. Seldom enthusiastic and interested

III. Knowledge in subject matter
   1. Excellent
   2. Good
   3. Average
   4. Poor
   5. Very Poor

IV. Instructor's ability to convey meaning of subject matter
   1. Consistently clear
   2. Usually clear
   3. Sometimes clear
   4. Seldom clear
   5. Unclear

V. General evaluation of teacher
   1. Excellent
   2. Good
   3. Average
   4. Poor
   5. Very Poor

VI. How would you rate the use of the Bible in this course?
   1. Very strong
   2. Strong
   3. Fair
   4. Weak
   5. Poor

VII. How practical or helpful has this course been for your Christian life?
   1. Very helpful
   2. Helpful
   3. Somewhat helpful
   4. Not very helpful

VIII. Organization of lessons
   1. Lessons consistently well organized, very easy to follow
   2. Lessons usually well organized, easy to follow

    3. Average organization of lessons, not too hard to follow
    4. Poor organization of lesson, somewhat disjointed
    5. Lessons disorganized and difficult to follow

IX. Use of class discussion
    1. Excellent use of class discussion
    2. Good use of class discussion
    3. Average use of class discussion
    4. Poor use of class discussion
    5. Not applicable

X. General evaluation of this course
    1. Superior in most respects
    2. Above average
    3. Average
    4. Below average

Are there any comments (either positive or negative) that you would like to make regarding your teacher?

Are there comments (either positive or negative) that you would like to make regarding this course?

Did the course in general meet your expectations? Please comment.

VII

ADULT LEARNING OPPORTUNITIES OTHER THAN SUNDAY

Drop by any night at First Busy Church and you are likely to find something happening. Sunday evening, the Divorce Recovery Group meets, eight weeks at a time, four times a year. Monday evening, a special Bible study involves small groups and intensive study. Tuesday evening, the lay counseling training takes place. Wednesday evening, fifteen to eighteen different classes are offered on a variety of subjects. Thursday evening, a special women's study group meets. Friday belongs to the singles group and two Twelve Step groups. Saturday features an all-day seminar on financial planning and stewardship. Sunday, it starts all over again.[1]

Not all adult learning can or should occur in the traditional Sunday morning setting. Sunday morning primarily builds fellowship and secondarily addresses learning. Sometimes, however, adults want to reverse this emphasis. Meeting the variety of human needs means a variety of education programs. Fitting into the diverse schedules of modern day people leads to class times outside the normal Sunday morning structures. Our hypothetical Busy Church has programs going on literally every night—and probably during the day, too. People in retirement and young mothers not working fill the daytime activities. Singles and working parents flock to the evening classes. People who work on weekends come to mid-week opportunities, and the "nine-to-five" folks populate the weekend activities. The specific-content courses reach out to meet the different needs and tastes of the congregation.

These courses last anywhere from a few hours to a few weeks. Some target very specific needs. Some offer training, connecting people with the demands of specific ministries. Others address particular interests. We can best classify these non-Sunday events through the needs each addresses.

Intensive Bible Studies

Intensive Bible studies for adults present a rapidly growing and significant form of adult learning in the church today. Several alternatives exist—from the *Disciples Bible Study* of The United Methodist Church to *Precepts,* an inductive study offered by a parachurch organization.[2]

All these studies make high demands on the participants. They require regular attendance at weekly meetings. Between meetings each person engages in lengthy study of assigned passages. Most people spend several hours a week in preparation for the class.

The meetings themselves take varying forms. Sometimes, the Bible study is a lecture given to a large group by a trained teacher. Other times the teaching comes through a video lecture. In either case, the lecture or teaching coordinates with a small group experience where the students discuss a prepared set of questions. The emphasis is not simply on Bible knowledge but the application of the Bible to personal life.

The growth and expansion of these intensive Bible study formats reflect the attraction of Bible study for many individuals. Part of the power of these studies comes from the small group dynamics, but do not discount the ongoing influence of Scripture for the lives of the people.

Intensive Bible studies attract a select group of people who enjoy the work and research. For this reason, offering a special class works better than making the intensive format part of the regular Sunday curriculum. Those who participate in the intensive format reflect a deep commitment to their faith. Some will have potential as teachers or for other leadership tasks.

Personal Growth Classes

Bill was in the midst of a painful divorce. One of his friends at work suggested that he try a group at church for newly divorced people. Desperate for anyone who would listen and care, Bill showed up hesitantly for the first session of the Divorce Recovery Class. He soon found that everyone there was hurting as he hurt. He talked, and they listened sympathetically. They talked, and he began to understand better what was happening to him. The group on Sunday night soon became a real lifeline for sanity in the midst of a very troubling time.

Bill is fictional, but his situation is not. The group he experienced falls under the general category of personal growth groups. This large subject area contains a variety of classes that focus on particular personal needs. The wide range of topics include everything from communication courses for couples to courses on prayer and spiritual formation.

The quality of personal growth groups depends on the quality of the bridge built between human needs and resources to meet those needs. These resources include video courses, people with special expertise from within the church, and people with expertise from outside. The needs reflected in these courses span the whole of human experience: family life and parenting, dealing with death and dying, personal finances, personal spiritual growth, setting goals, and changing life habits—the list is as long as the church's resources and imagination.

Local churches offer these courses at varying times and in differing formats. Classes meet afternoons, weekends, and every evening of the week. The resources for courses come from many sources. One church recruited people from the local hospice to offer courses on grief, the spiritual formation teacher from the local Roman Catholic diocese to offer courses on spiritual classics, a video program from a parachurch organization on personal budgeting and stewardship, local college professors and teachers to offer specialized courses, and their own staff and laity for courses on counseling, prayer, and family life. Local schools, junior colleges, hospitals, and counseling services have a wealth of people with the ability to teach a short course on a subject of interest to people in any church.

Ministry Training Courses

Short-term adult courses also provide opportunities for training people for ministry outreach. If the church has an evangelistic ministry, courses exist for training people in visitation and faith sharing. Similarly, when churches send people on short-term missions programs, some sort of training program helps deal with the issues of ministry in another culture. Short courses for teachers help motivate adult, children, and youth workers. Whatever ministries exist in your church can and should be undergirded through non-Sunday training events.

We called our Wednesday night program "LIFE-FM" (Lay Institute For Equipping For Ministry) to emphasize a commitment to training laity for ministry. Every Wednesday night we offered between fifteen to twenty courses, many directly related to lay ministry. The lay-counseling ministry encompassed some two hundred volunteers, and required courses for participation in that ministry met Wednesday night. Similarly, we scheduled courses for people considering missionary service, courses to train our lay evangelists, and courses for lay pastors.

The amount of training required for a ministry varies according to the need. The lay-counseling courses required extensive training—up to one hundred and fifty classroom hours. The lay-evangelist courses normally required a six-week course, one hour per week. Whatever the ministry, we made clear links between the training offered and the ministry—and Wednesday night was the place for most (though not all) of this training. The emphasis on training allowed us to stress the importance of lay ministry, gave confidence to our volunteers, and helped to facilitate recruiting.

Training courses have one major potential pitfall: Training for ministry does not mean doing ministry. Some people take the training and never do the ministry. Ministry training that disconnects the classroom from the experience of doing ministry often falls short. Thus, the best of these courses provide ministry experience early in the course as well as instruction.

Another form of ministry training focuses on the aptitude and motivation people bring to ministry, rather than on creating ministry skills. The Networking Class offered in many churches—most notably Willow Creek Community Church—takes members through a number of lessons wherein they identify their spiritual gifts, their personality patterns (based on a modified version of the Myers-Briggs inventory), their motivations, and their skills, and then seeks to match these with a list of job descriptions of ministries in the church.[3]

The Networking course helps people match themselves with the ministry for which they are already most gifted and motivated. Once the person links with the ministry, further training occurs "on the job" through the ministry leaders. This overcomes the major weakness of classroom training by placing the person in the ministry as they are trained. On the downside, however, this apprenticeship approach limits the depth and breadth of the classroom training.

Membership Classes

Many churches develop a specific and intensive set of courses for new members. Since more and more people grow up without a strong church heritage, leaders can no longer assume members have picked up the basics of the faith somewhere in children's or youths' Sunday school. Therefore, training in what it means to be a Christian, how to study the Bible, and how to walk out one's faith have become a major part of many church programs.

Saddleback Valley Community Church in Mission Viejo, California, has developed an intentional and thoughtful system for training its many new converts. The church offers four courses which lead the new believer in understanding and applying her or his faith:

Discovering Church Membership—a four-hour membership class giving the basics of Christian faith and defining what church membership means.

Discovering Spiritual Maturity—a second course that discusses means of developing the believer's individual commitment and spiritual maturity.

Discovering My Ministry—a course that helps the believer find his or her spiritual gifts, motivations, abilities, personality, and experiences (personal, educational, vocational, spiritual), and begin a personal ministry.

Discovering My Mission—a course that helps people develop a world vision, a commitment to sharing their faith, and a mission for their lives.

Each of these classes occurs on a Sunday afternoon. The courses seek to take the individual through a series of learning experiences that both define and apply the meaning of the Christian faith while integrating the person into the church and ministry. Some of this overlaps with the Networking course discussed earlier. Good membership courses should do more than just teach people about the faith—these courses can be a means of integrating faith and life.[4]

The How and When of Setting Up Non-Sunday Courses

To set up any non-Sunday course, someone must decide what needs will be met and by whom. If you are going to train for ministry, what ministries? If you are going to focus on personal growth courses, what needs will they meet?

Once you have focused on the type of training the church most wants to take up, the "when" depends on when the people needing the course can come. Putting together a program that meets several groups of needs at one setting greatly strengthens the program.

Many churches have found that combining training and personal growth courses for adults with a very fine children's program, the adult choirs, and a youth program gives families a venue in which all can participate during a given evening during the week. The evening will begin with an inexpensive dinner where families gather and eat together around tables. Then, the church will offer courses for the adults in one-hour and two-hour blocks. The children may have their choice of the choir program or a Bible study club. The youth generally break into small groups for discipleship, or go to nearby places for community ministry. The adult choir will meet after the first hour of classes.

Churches have traditionally used Wednesday night for these activities, but there is nothing sacrosanct about Wednesday evening. One church put together a similar program on Sunday evening. Yet another church offered its classes primarily during the day, appealing to retired people and those not on the job. Each church needs to survey its members to see what works best in that area, and have activities planned to coincide with the free time of their members and potential members.

Other types of courses fit best in a weekend or a more intensive format. Courses for engaged couples and marriage enrichment courses often take place during a long weekend. *Walk Through the Bible* offers an excellent weekend format for an introduction to inductive Bible study. Denominations often have courses that their staff members can bring to churches. Two or three special weekend emphases can greatly invigorate a congregation.

A tremendous variety of great educational experiences awaits any church. Bringing people together for these extra-Sunday times builds up their enthusiasm for the church, stretches their faith, creates new opportunities for ministry, and expands the congregation's horizons. Do not expect to get the same number outside of Sunday morning that you do on Sunday—we normally experienced about 45 percent of our Sunday morning Sunday school attendance on Wednesday night events. However, these people were the core of our Sunday morning leadership. As they grew in excitement about the different types of study we offered in the church, their enthusiasm spread, and more people came. Our non-Sunday morning adult learning provided depth for our overall program, and strengthened the Sunday morning program.

VIII

ADULT LEARNING IN THE SMALL CHURCH

A workshop leader was addressing a group of laity and pastors about the idea of rotating adult teachers and developing their own curriculum. Afterward, a group of pastors ganged up on him, "Do you really think this would work in a small church?" They asked, "How would you begin to implement these things in my church?"

Can a church with two or three adult classes, no professional staff, and limited resources really do what we have been describing? Without a doubt small churches with less than one hundred in attendance (and this takes in the majority of churches) face special challenges. Possibilities exist for expanding the educational ministry of the small church. But working in the small-church structure requires vision, patience, and leadership to effect significant changes.

Small Churches Are Different

In small churches, relationships and intimacy count more than numbers or vision. The pastor in a small church functions more as a chaplain. Leadership in small churches means lay leadership. Most small churches look mainly to preserve the traditions of the past and take care of the people there.[1] Growth for its own sake may not interest the average small congregation.

Small churches face several challenges in changing or growing an adult education program:

Small churches get very few visitors. When we talk about forming new classes, a small church might ask, "from among whom?" Small churches often function as clans and consist of a few significant families and friends. Therefore, most of the friendship networks represented in the people of the church already exist within the church. The opportunity to do something new with new people does not exist.

Adult classes in small churches tend to be made up of older adults. Rural churches especially have fewer younger families—many of whom have moved out of the area, leaving mainly older members of the clan in the church. The adult classes, therefore, consist of older adults who have known one another a long time and have an established format that they like. Again, the potential for change and growth does not appear to exist.

Small churches lack leadership resources. People with communication skills and teaching ability are either already teaching or simply not visible in many small churches. The idea of finding people who teach well, and who might develop their own curriculum, seems unlikely.[2]

Where There Is Life, There Is Hope

Small churches sometimes feel that there simply is not much they can do to change things. But reality may be different from perception. A young pastor told me of a process she went through with a small church. The church board members told her, "There simply is not much room for growth here; everyone we know is already in some church." Rather than take that statement at face value, the pastor had the board list every church in the county. Then they estimated attendance and membership for each church. Finally, they compared the numbers they gathered for church attendance and membership with the population numbers for the city and county. The astounded board discovered that only half their county and city attended church. The other half of the people in their city were potential churchgoers—if they had some reason to go. At that point the board members became much more receptive to ideas about changing their approach to education.

Members of small churches may assume that people who want to come to church will get there without being asked. "If people aren't in church, they don't want to be there," they often say. But according to Gallup Poll information, about one-half of all unchurched people say that they could see themselves going to church.[3] Of those who came back to church, simply being asked was an important factor for about one in six. Other issues were a sense of inner need to go back to church, the desire to rediscover one's faith, and the desire to get religious training for their children.[4] A good adult class addresses these inner issues of meaning and faith. To put it simply, the potential for reaching people does exist, if churches want to reach them.

Changing Perceptions in a Small Church

The pastor mentioned above helped create the possibility for change through educating her board. Education is always a key ingredient in beginning new programs in a small church. Most small churches feel comfortable with themselves. They know and like one another pretty well. The status quo already satisfies most of their relational needs. Therefore, little felt need for change exists.

Change comes when people believe that the benefits of the change outweigh the costs of change.[5] To initiate change, people must sense the need for change, accept that the cost of change is relatively small, and feel that the benefits of the change are worth it. The key people involved in the change must be brought on board and believe in what is being done. The fears many have about change call for discussion and care.

In terms of the small church, changing the adult learning program means gathering together a core of people who have vision for improving adult classes and offering opportunities for growth. Here is where "change agents" involved with the small church need patience. Leaders in small churches need a chance to believe in the possibility of reaching new people and the desirability of doing so. When people both know and experience the benefits of doing things differently, change becomes possible.

One small rural church began to change and grow when a few of the members began to go on "Volunteer in Missions" trips. The trips exposed the members to people very different from themselves. Despite these differences in culture and language, the American church people found themselves making deep friendships with new people around their common Christian faith. Once they learned the joy of making new friends far away from home, the American Christians applied the lesson to their situation back home. They looked for new people close at hand and the church began to grow.

Preaching and teaching can reinforce the experience people get through these contacts. As long as the needs of people outside the church remain abstract pictures in the minds of members, change will be hard. Once church people meet real people-needs face to face and experience something new themselves, change becomes possible.

Develop a Core of Leaders

The critical need for teachers and leaders in small churches defeats most attempts to improve the adult classes. Therefore, developing leaders must come in advance of any significant change.

At the same time, just such an action may create problems in a small church. One pastor pointed out, "If you start a small group to develop leaders, you may alienate those who aren't in the group." The small church often expects the pastor to be a chaplain: That means he or she visits everyone, cares for the whole flock, and does the ministry. This can imply that no one gets special treatment from the pastor.

Two possible solutions can overcome this threat. First, a denominational program like *Disciples* Bible study offers a great vehicle for leadership development without the threat of seeming like special treatment for a few. When people spend a number of weeks together, studying and thinking about the Christian faith, some will begin to evidence leadership skills and teaching ability. A program like *Disciples* Bible study will also draw in committed and available people. The joy of meeting together and studying together becomes contagious. Those who find faith a serious and joyful adventure will want to share this experience with others. The experience of these people opens up the possibility of new educational programs in the church. Since the program comes from the denomination, people may accept it without blaming the pastor for giving special treatment to a few.

Second, leadership development can work when the present church leadership owns the ideas as their own. Programs that come only from the pastor struggle in any church. The small church simply magnifies this fact.[6] The pastor can lay the groundwork by working with the present leadership of the church and letting them begin to wrestle with the problem and develop solutions. The pastor can encourage church leaders to discuss critical questions: Where will the future of the church be? Where can we find future leadership? Where are our friends and family who are not in the church? How can we get them in? The leadership may or may not commit to much direct help in solving these problems, but at least permission may be given to try.

At the same time, the pastor remains an important, though often underused, resource for some small churches. Often, pastors in smaller churches have no teaching responsibilities. Not all pastors teach well, but pastors may offer new leadership possibilities for the smaller church.[7] The pastor has received training both in theology and speaking that should make her or him a person prepared to teach. Similarly, a pastor who teaches in the adult classes adds status and importance to the education program by his or her presence. Finally, teaching helps the pastor further to deepen relationships with the people of the church and enhances the pastor's overall effectiveness.

Video series can also help overcome a lack of teaching resources. The video becomes the teacher. The church then needs a discussion facilitator, not someone who actually prepares the lesson. Typically, such videos provide some sort of study guide to help with this process.

Finding New People

Developing new leadership for the church is only half the problem. For most small churches, changes make little sense because too few new needs come into the church to make the change necessary. New needs and new people go hand in hand. Finding people means identifying their needs.

Knocking on doors is the old-fashioned, and still relevant, means of doing this. Steve Drury went to Grassland United Methodist Church as a student pastor. They expected to close the church before the end of that year. Thirteen years later, Steve is still there and the church averages more than two hundred in worship.

When asked how they did it, Steve answered, "We knocked on a lot of doors." The church was in a remote and rural location. Figuring that people lived in the area who did not attend any church, they simply went out and asked them to come.

The Grassland Church was so depleted in membership that the pastor faced little resistance to asking new people in. In other churches with fifty or so in attendance, however, the members may not want some of their neighbors to come. But the point still remains—you can find new people if you ask them to come. Developing a willingness to ask may take time and persuasion, but once you ask, response is possible. A line in a recent movie told us, "If you build it, they will come." But, "Ask them to come, and they will build it" can be equally true.

Churches can also find new people by running short-term programs. A video series that features a popular topic or a well-known figure, offered at night to the general public, can draw people in for a first look at a church. In the last session, ask for an evaluation of the program and check for interest in future offerings. Follow up with these programs in the future and offer Sunday morning opportunities to those interested. Huge numbers may not respond, but the nucleus for a new class can emerge.

Social events can also provide opportunities for reaching new people. A barbecue or a bean supper for the neighborhood will bring out new people. Invite people either by going door to door or by passing out circulars. The event could include entertainment and other types of fun, but it should probably not be used for specific evangelistic appeals. Rather, the purpose is to focus on developing relationships and presenting the church as a friendly place to come. Opportunities for new adult classes can be presented.

Special events for children and youth also draw new families to a church. One small neighborhood church advertised its Vacation Bible School around the neighborhood and found some new families who were interested in the church. A youth event or retreat can similarly find people if you let them know what is going on.

Rotating Teachers and Developing Your Own Curriculum

Do the ideas of rotating teachers and developing a unique curriculum help the smaller church? Yes, although I would not expect either to happen overnight. Rotating teachers makes sense to the smaller church for the same reason as to the larger church: Teachers get more out of less preparation when they teach short courses in more than one class. When the pastor teaches, rotating from class to class gives her or him greater exposure to the whole church. Rotating the teachers continues to make sense even if we are talking about only two or three adult classes.

However, classes that have enjoyed the same teacher for many years will not normally want to change. These classes will have to begin seeing good results before they are willing to go along with a new approach. Example: Let us assume that the church has three adult classes, only one of which will try the rotation idea. Through short-term courses or special events, the church may recruit new people to start another class. Begin the rotation idea with just these two classes. Instead of six two-month courses, perhaps consider sticking with a three-month curriculum for the time being. If the pastor teaches, the teacher of the existing class agrees to teach, and you add one new teacher and one video course (with a discussion leader), then you have a four-course rotation available. This creates a system with diversity and change in which each teachers gets at least six months off from teaching. Each course might even have an apprentice working with the teacher or discussion leader, as a means of developing new leadership for the future.

This showcases the idea of changing teachers and courses for the other classes. Classes, of course, may still not want to change their format. Some, however, will see the possibilities. Classes can choose to participate or not, depending on the goals and personality of the class.

Small churches cannot do everything at once. What we have described is a process. But the process in the small church parallels the process in the larger church. What needs exist to which our church could be in ministry? What resources do we have to meet those needs? How can we invite people to classes and courses in which they as individuals can grow in the faith? How can we make the curriculum relevant and the teaching load workable for our people? These questions relate to all sizes of churches. The process of change will be different in a small church because the relational issues differ. Small churches move by love and concern and not so much by management, but the tools we have described in the first several chapters will help the smaller church when applied with love and sensitivity.

IX

ROOMS AND EQUIPMENT FOR ADULT LEARNING

Speaking to a group of executive ministers of large churches, Lyle Schaller once said, "The first thing I do when I go into a church is to notice the smell." The look, feel, and yes, smell of a building matter to people. New theaters fill up; old theaters sit empty. New malls draw customers in droves. Older stores either move, remodel, or close.

Dank, dark rooms are not impossible settings for an adult class, but they discourage all but the most committed. The environment of a class either helps or hinders the spirit of the class. Newcomers tend to evaluate a situation based on the setting. First impressions powerfully influence future behaviors. In addition to the discussion that follows, you may want to read *First Impressions: How to Present an Inviting Church Facility* by Robert Lee for suggestions on how to improve the physical environment of your church.

Room Size

I was sitting in my office doing some last minute preparation across the hall from the class I was teaching. My office door was open, and I saw a couple come up to the classroom door and look in. As they spoke quietly to each other, one said, "There's no room." And then they left. Curious, I got up and went to the classroom door. I counted at least eight empty chairs among approximately one hundred in the room. It was *not* technically full, but it looked full. What was more important was that it *felt* full to the newcomers. So, they left.

When I started working with adult classes, I was told that most church groups stabilize attendance at about 80 percent of room capacity. We tested this theory several times. The "One in the Spirit" class, for example, met in a room that held 60 chairs. The class attendance averaged 45 to 50 persons each Sunday. Since they were in an age group (30 to 40) that promised growth potential and had good leadership, we moved them to a larger class to give them the chance to grow. Their new room held 90 chairs. Within 18 months, average attendance increased to about 70. After three or four years, we decided to try another room, this time with the capacity for 120 chairs. Again, within two years the class was averaging between 90 to 100 and more. Each move led to a growth spurt that leveled out at about 80 percent of room capacity.

The growth of the class was not as simple as changing the room size. Without strong leadership, an open personality that welcomed new people, and good teaching, they would not have grown. However, if we had left them in their original room, they would not have grown. Unless a room contains more than 20 percent empty chairs, newcomers conclude that there is no space for them.

Empty seats also send a message to present class members—we need more people. Classes can very easily become comfortable staying in their known social networks. A filled room and crowded space diminish the felt need in the class to involve new people. The self-satisfaction of the class becomes an additional barrier. Few people will force themselves into a group where they are not wanted or invited. Ample space for growth encourages classes to welcome people. Crowded rooms deter that behavior.

Too much space also presents a problem. The New Covenant class averaged about 40 to 50 people per week. The class had good leadership, effective outreach, and a friendly spirit. But members felt frustrated. Their classroom, which could hold 140 people, was set up for the large class that met the previous hour. The New Covenant class filled less than half the chairs set up. They were a healthy class, but the vast numbers of empty chairs kept saying to them, "Where is everyone?" Attitude and morale improved when the class moved to a smaller room.

The "perfect" room for a class with growth potential has 25 to 40 percent more chairs than needed. Much more than 40 percent extra capacity is defeating; less than 20 percent turns people away. A survey of your adult class space will reveal how much potential for growth the classes have.

Many churches build classrooms that will hold around twenty adults. Small wonder that most adult classes average around fifteen. Is there anything wrong with small classes? Small classes provide wonderful intimacy for members. The friendship and caring should not be discounted. However, do newcomers today want this sort of intimacy? Many baby boomers and others who grew up in large schools and large classes find larger groups less threatening than small groups. They want to come and "be" in a group before participating. In a small class, everyone has a job. Many people today like to be in groups where they can assume responsibility but also have the opportunity to sit back from time to time and let someone else do it. This happens more easily in classes that average thirty or more in attendance. Additionally, changes in the membership of a small class cause a greater upheaval in the class dynamics than do membership changes in a larger class. In a small class one couple moving out of town may make a major difference. Larger classes have a larger pool of people for leadership and more resilience in dealing with the change that emanates from the job relocations typical of modern life.

The ideal: Have as much *flexible* space as possible in the adult learning area. This allows classes to grow, or shrink, and allows leaders to place them in the best possible space. Buildings, especially older buildings, offer limited flexibility. But if the church has reached a plateau or has a declining adult learning program, one part of an effective diagnosis is an examination of room size. Can you move classes with potential for growth into space that allows growth? If not, can you find or build such space? Creating larger learning spaces, and relocating classes with potential for growth will be critical for the long-term development of adult classes.

Two other space considerations confront us. First, we must reckon with the fact that people expect more space today. Lyle Schaller points out that the average house in 1948 was 748 square feet. Today, people with smaller families probably expect twice that square footage to feel comfortable.[1] This suggests that the educational space of the 1950s and 1960s probably serves fewer people today than when originally built—because the amount of space needed per person has increased. Staying the same physical size probably means growing smaller.

Second, churches need to see adult space as both social space and educational space. Measure a classroom by the space for socializing, drinking coffee, and talking as well as in terms of its seating capacity. Classes need social space. So the true capacity of a room goes beyond the number of chairs you can cram into the space.

Classroom Decor

Only the most dedicated would tolerate some of our classrooms. Worn carpet, thirty-year-old couches (that were second-hand to begin with), bare walls, and poor lighting do not welcome or inspire adults. If the local bank or the local doctor's office looked like some adult classroom space, who would come?

The church needs a plan for the *look* of its rooms. Consider forming an interior design task force to make recommendations to the trustees for paint, carpet, and furnishings for classrooms. You want nicely painted walls with up-to-date colors. The out-of-date color schemes scream a message to newcomers: We do not know or care what is going on today. Repaint the walls on a regular schedule, and use this as a time to liven up the colors. Replace the carpet, too, before it gets old and tattered. Good advice—professional, if possible—on these types of selections is worth the effort. Going with the advice of a professional not only keeps the church current in decor but avoids personal disputes over the tastes of church members.

Give some thought to the comfort of your classes. Chairs can add or detract. The hard metal type lasts forever, but afflicts the user. Chairs with cushions look better and feel better but present maintenance problems. Concentrate on comfort and appearance where possible, while remembering that the need to rearrange the Sunday setting for other uses must also be taken into account.

Most of what we have said is common sense. Churches often fail to plan maintenance because of a money shortage. But short-term savings have long-terms costs. Ideally, a local church should figure on some minor remodeling and upgrading of decor each year. The best maintenance comes a bit at a time.

Adult classes will often help finance their own room maintenance and upkeep. But be aware of the dangers in having classes maintain their own rooms. After they provide the money for remodeling a room, class members naturally tend to view the room as "theirs." This makes them want to stay there forever. If the class grows too large for the space, it will resist moving. If another class needs the space more, the "owners" may want to stay despite the needs of others. If other groups want to use the space outside of the adult Sunday school hours, these classes will sometimes resist sharing their space.

No class should feel that it "owns" any room. The church as a whole maintains an interest in a room when the general budget shares at least part of any expense encountered in remodeling. Where possible, the church should ensure that the personal effects of the class (such as pianos, songbooks, cabinets, or podiums) remain portable. If the class can take its identity with it, then the church retains the ability to move classes. This maximizes the use of space without undermining class spirit.

Beware of "gifts" to the class (but not to the church). The strings attached to the gift may cause problems. One member of a class wanted to donate a sound system, but only on the condition that the class maintain the exclusive use of the system. After trying (and failing) to negotiate a means of protecting the equipment while allowing for general use of the system, the leaders politely passed on the gift. Eventually, they found a way to provide the needed sound system for all the groups that used the room, rather than tie the system and the room down to one class.

Making classrooms as comfortable as possible, as attractive as possible, and as socially inviting as possible creates the right atmosphere for adult classes. In existing facilities this takes time. Create a plan for remodeling the rooms a few at a time over four to five years. Beginning a process of improving the facilities will help the morale and effectiveness of classes greatly.

Teaching Media

A visitor dropped by a small, independent TV studio in Shreveport, Louisiana. There he saw the production of a class going live via satellite into hundreds of classrooms across the country. As the show was going on, students called in by phone to ask questions of the presenters. An unusual event? No, the same type of program happens daily in dozens of locations. Video, TV, and computers no longer pass as innovative teaching tools. Teaching more and more assumes the availability of technology as a tool.

Look at the closest and newest elementary school building, and you are likely to see the latest in "hi-tech" equipment. Each class probably has a bank of computers and a TV monitor that is connected to the library from which films, tapes, and educational television can be sent on demand to the individual classroom. Each room has phone lines that can connect by modem with other computer and video systems across the state and the nation. A mix of teaching media will be standard fare from now on. The church will be left behind if it settles for a chalkboard in a teleprompter age.

Hi-tech equipment will invade (and already has to some degree) the world of Sunday school classes. A few sensible purchases of teaching equipment can help even churches of modest means greatly improve their teaching. This would include:

* Sound systems for larger classrooms
* Marker boards/chalkboards
* Screens
* Overhead projectors
* Video players and monitors

Smaller classes, of course, do not require sound systems. But larger classrooms (with more than 60 people) will function better with a good system. Older members, too, appreciate being able to hear teachers. This need not be an elaborate system, but something simple and easily installed. A good combination public address system/cassette recorder costs about $500. Having bought the equipment, carefully consider how to secure and store it; thieves love sound equipment.

Many teachers enjoy using a chalkboard or marker board. The latter is becoming the more favored tool, since it eliminates the mess of chalk and allows the use of erasable and colorful pens. The board should be properly located (so that the normal set up of the class faces the board) and adequately sized. In older classrooms, or rooms where a permanent board is not desirable, portable boards should be made available. This requires a central location for distributing marker and materials to teachers and classes on Sunday.

The overhead projector offers advantages over the old chalkboard and the new marker board. A screen in the classroom is less obtrusive than a board. The overhead projector allows the teacher to write on the projector surface and face the class at the same time. Teacher and class interaction improves greatly when the teacher maintains eye contact. Firms that provide materials for overhead projectors often will offer basic instruction in the use of the machines for your teachers.

Churches probably cannot justify the cost of the sophisticated central systems for voice and video that many schools are installing. However, churches can buy a TV monitor, a VCR machine, and a portable stand to hold them. This can be moved from class to class as needed. Not every room needs a TV monitor and VCR (providing security and storage is an important issue). In 1990, however, 49 percent of all churches had computers (most for administrative and financial services), and 68 percent had VCRs. By the year 2000 projections suggest that 83 percent of all churches will have computers, and 89 percent will have VCRs.[2] Children are growing up in schools that make increasingly sophisticated use of both computers and visual media. Churches that take advantage of these technological developments will have the edge in attracting the adult learners of the future.

Can a church really afford these tools? Many of these pieces of equipment are not expensive: A VCR/monitor combination may cost less than $500; an overhead projector costs between $200 and $400; a marker board costs between $100 and $500 depending on size. Most of this equipment can be moved from class to class as it is needed. Therefore, the church does not have to justify spending a thousand dollars or more to equip a single classroom used only Sunday morning at 9:30. Moreover, if a church is looking at extending its educational program to more than one hour and more than Sunday morning, these types of investments make more and more sense. Most churches will want to plan a long-term process for buying and using equipment in order to spread out the cost. Once equipment is available, more and more uses for teaching and learning will be discovered. Seek to purchase industrial-grade rather than commercial-grade equipment where possible. The industrial grade will handle movement better and usually has fewer features (therefore, less that can go wrong).[3]

Once the classes have the equipment, the church will want to examine the possibility of purchasing or renting video and audio tapes and overhead projector materials. Often, denominational offices have materials that local congregations can borrow. This allows the church to try some material before beginning to develop its own library. Book distributors and parachurch ministries offer material for purchase and rental. In most cases, purchasing makes sense when you expect to use the material more than once.

The use of media in adult learning in the church will grow and change in coming years. As more and more of the TV generation makes up each congregation, mixed media will reach people better than the old quarterly lesson and discussion method. These materials can make teaching and learning more interesting and more relevant, and smart churches will plan ahead to make better use of the media at hand.

X

SINGLES CLASSES ARE DIFFERENT— AND NOT

Each week, the members of the staff received a copy of the new-member list. And just about every week Mel, the Minister of Family Life and Singles, said, "Look at the number of singles who are joining! At least one-third of all our new members are singles. We have to do a better job of meeting their needs if we are going to keep them."

The statistics are undeniable. People are waiting later to get married.[1] Approximately half of all marriages end in divorce. Singles make up more and more of our society. If singles are different from married couples in their needs and expectations, then this growing group of people need special attention.

But are they really different? The answer is yes and no. As a group, singles do differ from nonsingles. Singles attend worship less frequently than married couples (39 percent to 57 percent), go less frequently to adult classes (14 percent to 29 percent), volunteer less (19 percent to 27 percent), and reduce their giving faster in times of recession (30 percent to 25 percent). Singles agree more strongly than marrieds with the statement, "Your first responsibility is to yourself" (33 percent to 23 percent). We find relatively few singles in church leadership positions (9 percent to 19 percent).[2] Some might conclude from these statistics that singles are the least dependable and least profitable group in the church.

The numbers, however, do not tell the whole story. Since singles include individuals like widows and widowers and single parents, we should not be surprised that they are more economically sensitive than other groups. Yet in times of economic recession, the majority of singles would first cut back spending on themselves before they would reduce spending on charity.[3] Within their context, singles give as generously as couples. And, since being single often comes as a part of some other transition in life (going into the work force, leaving a marriage, losing a mate), we should not be surprised that their lives reflect more change overall than married people.

Singles want the same things in a church as married couples.[4] They prefer a friendly church that features good teaching for themselves and their children. When they find this, singles invite their friends more frequently than do married couples (57 percent to 52 percent).[5]

Put all this fragmentary information together, and what does it suggest?

* Singles are increasing in numbers.
* Singles are less likely to be in church.
* Singles can be hard to reach.
* Singles come to church when singles invite them.
* Singles are attracted by the same things that attract married couples: good worship, good teaching, good classes for their children, and a caring atmosphere.

Are singles different? Yes, singles are different in that they are dealing with special transitions in life—out of college or out of a marriage through divorce or through the death of a spouse. And, yes, singles are different in the sense that some singles have special tensions in their lives: the burden of single-parenting, dealing with household finances, or new duties due to being alone again after years of a partnership. Churches have traditionally organized around family structure, leaving singles to feel odd and out of place. But singles are not really different in what they are looking for in a church: fellowship

114

resources, encouragement, and direction in their lives. Single people, like all people, expect the church to provide a forum for their own discovery of God's meaning for their lives. Adult classes for singles need to provide teaching, fellowship, and ministry for single adults in terms of the special emphases of the single life.[6]

Four Types of Singles

We cannot speak of "singles" as if all singles were alike. At least four separate groups of singles exist in any church: the never-been-married, the longer-term single person, the divorced, and the widowed.

Each of these groups has a different self-perception and a different set of needs. The never-been-married group is typically younger, very energetic, and positive (you may or may not include college students here). Members of this group may resist the tag of "single," since they see themselves more as "pre-married" people rather than specifically single. They orient themselves around careers and developing relationships. Having just taken charge of their lives, members of the "pre-married" class may not want anything extra from the church except the chance to run their own class. They will be especially interested in insights regarding early career decisions and preparation for marriage (the latter in small doses, since they may not be in a hurry to get married). They may enjoy teachers who can also function as mentors, but they will want to develop their own leadership.

The volatility of such classes poses the major challenge of working with this group. The strongest leaders in the class tend to marry first and move on to a newlywed class. Many will be in their first job and may be forced to make career moves. This group includes graduate students who will finish school and move. These classes have trouble maintaining consistent leadership, and over time may die out.

The long-term singles may not fit into any one group. For various reasons these people have never married, but they have moved past the early questions of career and beginning job decisions. They may or may not be actively pursuing marriage options. Most long-term singles are seeking to establish or maintain a worthwhile identity as a single person in the midst of a world of couples.

Members of this group of singles have a significant amount of time and commitment to give and are looking for places of ministry. Long-term singles often mix in with the other groups of singles, rather than finding their own group. They seem to be group-joiners rather than group-formers. Once the group forms, long-term singles provide service and even leadership to the class.

The divorced persons in a congregation make up the third group of singles. The growth of and the needs of this group have become very familiar in our society. Pain and loss come with divorce. People who come to the church after a divorce are almost always looking for healing and assurance. Having lost the major relationship in their lives, they are looking for companionship and friendship. But they may also be experiencing financial pressures, stress with family and children, and sometimes relocation. Many are not ready to give much in terms of leadership and commitment. Their focus is on receiving help and healing.

Not surprisingly, developing leadership becomes a prime concern for these classes. People who are not so newly divorced are needed to step up into leadership for these classes and provide continuity. The minister, a staff person, or a volunteer must provide time and effort to supporting and encouraging the leadership of the class.[7] Not that this means doing everything for this group—leadership can and must develop within the group. But, especially at the beginning, some special source of leadership will need to provide organization and energy to facilitate the group.

Widows and widowers form the final group. They can be the "silent" group of singles in a church. Most will already be part of an adult class. If a spouse dies after retirement, a widow or widower usually stays in his or her present adult class because many in the class will be going through the same experience. Those who lose their spouse at an early age may go (permanently or part-time) to a singles group in order to meet other single people.

The loss of a spouse at any time traumatizes the survivor. However, the grief of losing a spouse to death differs from that of divorce. Readjustments must be made, but the friendship network is more easily maintained. If the surviving spouse has been the caretaker of a wife or husband with a long-term, debilitating illness, he or she may now have time and energy to spend on other projects. The surviving spouse needs care and support, but normally at a level and intensity different from the divorced person.

The differences in these four groups suggest that the church needs to have not one, but several, emphases for singles. The never-been-married group will focus on initial career decisions and initial relationships. Divorced persons seek encouragement and healing. Widowed persons look for support and friendship. The long-term single will want to find friendship and meaningful activities. Certain social events will draw all the groups together, but often their interests go in different directions.

The Large Network Singles Class

A number of good models exist in which one large single adult class serves the whole single population. In one sense, these operate on the model of the old Sunday school structure. A large assembly including all singles begins the morning. This is a time of singing, sharing, general announcements, and prayer. The assembly then splits into smaller classes for specific courses. These courses cover a number of topics of concern to singles—especially personal and spiritual growth and relationships—and can vary in duration.

The very size of the large singles class gives it enviable durability. Leadership forever reemerges from within the class to keep the momentum going. The class gives people a variety of learning, social, and ministry opportunities. The format actively generates new events to meet needs and interests. As new people come, they are given opportunities to develop new ideas or social events or ministries. Leadership is therefore constantly being developed and renewed from within the class.

The class also serves the social needs of singles well. A constant flow of social events (with leadership from the class) provides numerous options for being with people. The continuing whirl of events offers people who are looking for something to do the options they seek. The large singles class excels as a place to meet people and be met.

The large singles class suffers less from the main challenge of singles ministry: the propensity of singles to move and change. The energy and social nature of the class constantly attract new people, and the openness of the class to new courses and new social events gives opportunity to the development of new leadership.

Averaging several hundred in attendance each week, the Phoenix class has existed since 1973 at a large church in the Midwest. The class has gone through several generations of leadership and carries on a very active social calendar. The Phoenix class has been very successful at attracting newly divorced people, providing a place for them to meet new people, and helping them find healing for the wounds of the past.

The problems of the large singles class correspond to its strengths. The class is somewhat self-sufficient—to the point that it may be poorly integrated into the rest of the church. Singles' needs and issues absorb the class so that, in effect, it becomes a separate organization. Therefore, the leadership of the class must be church members and part of the overall structure of the church.

Similarly, the social and relational strengths of the class may overwhelm spiritual issues. The social agenda of the class may drive the class so well that it becomes only nominally Christian. An intentional emphasis on spiritual topics in the courses and activities of the class will help bring balance to the overall program.[8]

A more practical problem exists for the large singles class model: this approach demands a large social and educational space for the program. Churches without a large area available to develop this program may be defeated from the start.

Multiple Singles Classes

Not all successful singles programs opt for the large "umbrella" format. Asbury United Methodist Church, also in Tulsa, Oklahoma, has a singles program that averages several hundred adults per Sunday in four classes. The four-class structure divides singles along stages-of-life lines:

* Early career singles: just out of college to about twenty-eight years old.
* Early thirties: about 50 to 60 percent have been married, but others are longer-term singles.
* Mid-thirties to mid-forties: singles who are largely parents of adolescents.
* Older singles: fifties and up, mostly people beyond the child-rearing stage, but now often dealing with aging parents.

This structure recognizes the different concerns of each group. The younger group concentrates on career and self-definition issues. The "thirties" group deals more with issues of divorce, single-parenting, and middle career. The parents of adolescents have their own concerns and issues, especially as single parents, which are different from parents of younger children. Singles whose children have grown up deal with issues such as caring for aging parents, career change, and relationships.

Leadership remains *the* issue for these classes. Creating a new singles class calls for an intentional leadership team that sets the tone for the class:

* Two co-leaders (always a man and a woman)
* A director of missions outreach
* A director of activities
* A director of outreach (pastoral care of the class)

The male and female co-leadership model makes an important statement.[9] In a singles class, each sex looks for someone in the leadership with whom to identify. Classes that have all-female leadership struggle to reach men (and I suspect the opposite would also be true). The up-front presence of both male and female leaders in the class suggests to newcomers that both men and women are valued and wanted within the class.

Relationships drive all classes, and especially singles classes. The Asbury leadership structure stresses this by having two persons who concentrate on developing relationships: one through social activities, and one through organizing caring. The emphasis on missions outreach gives the class a service outlet. But service projects also offer relational opportunities. A woman who directs a popular singles' ministry shared that one singles class at her church developed numerous community service activities that allow them to get together and work together. They work in housing projects, homes for the elderly, and other programs. The class members see these as opportunities both to do ministry and to be together as they do something worthwhile.

While the class leadership focuses on relationship and mission, the church provides the teaching. Teachers and content in the singles classes integrate the classes into the total church ministry. In this way the singles classes act less as an independent appendage to the church and more as a part of the whole church program.

A church I visited recently uses several "All-Singles" events to tie the classes together. Quarterly, all the singles classes meet on Sunday morning for a common assembly to hear a special teacher (not normally part of the regular teaching of the church). Once a year, they have a special "Thanksgiving" Sunday where the group recognizes volunteers and where people share their stories of God's grace in their lives. From time to time there are also all-singles social events or missions projects.

Making this kind of program work depends on the ability of the church to live with change. Singles classes constantly change and redefine themselves. As a class grows older, some people will resist that change and move down to a younger class, which may in turn create a need for a yet younger class.

As people in a singles class marry or move, classes will restructure and reform. The church must allow the class to find its own identity, and then allow that identity to change as the needs of the people change. For example, a class may begin as a college and career group, but over time evolve into a class of single parents.

Many churches find that every two years or so a new singles class must be created to replace one that faded away. Typically, a group of singles creates a class, and the class would grow. Then, people in the class would begin to marry and others would move, until the leadership pool becomes depleted. Frequently, newer singles in the church will prefer to start their own class rather than attempting to move into leadership roles in an established class. When this is the case, letting nature take its course proves wiser than trying to keep classes alive.

Integrating Singles into Other Classes

Not all churches like the idea of specific singles classes. Not all singles want to be in classes where one is identified as single. One church staff person declared, "Our singles are tired of being labeled 'single.' They prefer simply to be 'Christian,' and they join groups like anyone else."

This is easily done in the case of older adult classes. Often, in these classes as men and women become widowed, they prefer to stay with friends they have known for years. Enough widows and widowers exist in the class to create a natural subgroup of those who have lost their spouse in the class itself. The old ties of relationships and the new shared experience of losing a spouse keep the class together.

In younger adult classes, this sometimes generates a different result. Some people will choose to stay in a class of married couples despite losing a spouse (either to divorce or death). This may reflect the strength of friendship ties, or the relationship the children of the now single parent have with the children of other adults in the class. When this happens, the single person in the class sometimes becomes a point of relationship to bring other singles into the class.

The Builders class, for example, consists primarily of married couples in their forties, largely professionals and small business people or executives. Over time, a few of the Builders became single and stayed in the class. These people began to do things like form their own small group, which served to attract other singles. A single man or woman might come to the Builders class because he or she identified with business peers in the class, or a single parent might know other parents through children and school. The singles in the Builders class were able to create a subgroup in the class. The singles met together socially, went out to visit evangelistically for the church together, and engaged in other activities. In other words, they began to do the relational and outreach functions of a singles class within the overall structure of a larger class.

Integrating singles into existing classes works best where the church can identify singles who have strong existing links to a class. These people act as leaders for inviting other singles to join.

As with any class, the goal of this type of singles group should be to create relational opportunities and outreach experiences for the singles. These activities would be either in addition to the regular class functions, or a singles' version of the class activity. If the class has small groups, a small group can form around the single members. The singles can take charge of visiting other single adults for the class or the church. In addition to class retreats, the single members of the class can organize an additional retreat for themselves.

For this structure to work effectively, the singles subgroup has to remain a minority in the class and participate fully in the regular class activities. Integrating singles into nonsingles classes depends on these people having singleness as a secondary identity. If the group begins to have large numbers of people and a strong singles identity, creating an independent singles' class will be helpful. There is nothing wrong with this. Singles' classes help us focus efficiently on the perceived needs of a significant group of adults.

Single Classes Are Worth It!

Any of these models can work: the large single class, multiple singles classes built around age and stage in life, or integrating singles into other classes. Each model exists to relate to the special needs of a growing section of our adult population. Recognizing these needs and doing something to meet these needs helps people. Along with the joy of meeting the needs of single adults for relationship and care, churches find that these people provide energy and ministry to others. Churches that serve singles find that singles serve in turn.[10]

XI

SMALL GROUPS FOR ADULT LEARNING

In a meeting of twenty-eight executive pastors, all of whom were in charge of the program areas of their churches, one pastor asked the group, "How many of you have adult Sunday school programs?" About one-half did. He then asked, "Do the rest of you have small group programs?" Every church that did not have an adult Sunday school did have a small group program. Further discussion revealed some significant observations:

1. Most churches that had Sunday schools also had small groups. The small groups functioned largely as a smaller subsidiary of the Sunday classes. Among the twenty-eight churches represented, the total number of people involved either in small groups or an adult Sunday class averaged about 70 percent of Sunday worship attendance.

2. In churches without adult Sunday school classes the small groups performed the function of adult classes. Teaching, ministry, and fellowship flowed through the small group. These churches also averaged about 70 percent of their Sunday worship attendance in these small groups.

Therefore, these churches had either a large adult Sunday school with relatively few small groups, or large numbers of small groups and no adult classes. Both small groups and adult classes performed the same functions of providing a supportive community, ministry opportunities, and teaching. Both small groups and adult classes tended to reach about the same numbers of people.

The Advantages of Small Groups

The difference between an adult class and a small group generally reflects a change in time, location, and size. Small groups generally meet at times other than Sunday morning, in a private home rather than the church, and generally comprise from six to sixteen members. (Some adult classes are obviously this small but can be much larger.) Why do some churches focus on small groups rather than adult classes?

Small groups make economic sense. Building adult classroom space is expensive. In metropolitan areas land and building costs inhibit church investment in educational space. Small groups can meet in homes, and the church normally pays nothing for this space.

Small groups offer opportunities for lay leadership. Whereas an adult class will have one president or leader, every small group has a leader. Since there will be more small groups than adult classes, more leaders can be utilized. Motivated lay people want to be used in ministry, and small groups give them an effective forum.

Small groups also develop leadership. Each group leader has an assistant to share the load and to mentor for future leadership. Moreover, small group leaders learn to look for new people with leadership potential and to find a place for these new leaders.

Small groups get the church out into the community where non-Christians are. Because they are typically held in the homes of members, small groups are more readily accessible, both physically and emotionally, to some people than is the church building. Some people find a home easier to visit than a church building.

Finally, small groups focus better on the individual. Even a moderate-sized congregation sometimes overlooks people—failing to miss a person who has dropped out or gotten lost. But every person in a small group is known by name. The small group notices who is there and who is not, and takes the initiative to contact people.

Types of Small Groups

Small groups come in many shapes and forms—each with a different function. Which small group model a church encourages depends on the goals and dreams of the church. At least five types of small groups exist today:

1. *The Home Group* is a small group that functions mainly to provide a pastoral-care and ministry focus for persons in the church. Most of the groups are geographically based—that is, set up in a particular neighborhood and drawing roughly from a specific geographical area. Each group has a "lay pastor" whose job it is to lead the group and to stay in touch with the members of the group.

If one person in the group is sick or going through a difficult time, the lay pastor visits him or her and rallies the group to help that person. Groups also act to meet needs perceived in the community outside their own membership.

The group meeting consists mainly of singing, prayer, and study—with a strong stress on group worship. Groups generally do not have a specific curriculum, but the group does Bible study or other study as the leader directs. The connection to the church comes through a meeting that each group leader has with the pastor-staff representative in the local church. The "lay pastors" meeting offers ongoing training to the group leadership and communication with the other groups and the church at large.

2. *The Task-oriented Group* begins with ministry instead of fellowship or study. Each group begins out of members' common desire to tackle a perceived need in the community. When at least four persons in the church want to work on a particular concern, a Community Ministry group begins. The group

searches out resources already existing in the community that are working on the perceived need. The group meets with resource persons and decides on some concrete action to meet the need.

The Jobs First ministry group organized to help unemployed people find work. The early group meeting set two simple goals. First, the group sought to meet with persons seeking employment and to help them write resumes and follow job leads. Second, the group wanted to create a sharing group for job seekers to help deal with the stresses of unemployment.

The relational function of the group came in the midst of this ministry. As the Jobs First group met to plan the support group and develop job resources, they would share with one another and pray together. The Jobs First group became a source of Christian friendship and faith building in the midst of practical ministry.

The task-oriented group will change over time. In one model of the task-oriented group, individuals have a chance to change groups, create new groups, stay in a group, or drop out altogether every six months. Commitment to the task-oriented group is strictly "want to," not "have to." Therefore, from time to time some groups disappear as the need for which they were created disappears. Groups should disband when members lack a genuine enthusiasm for the ministry. Only in the context of a strong personal desire to do the ministry can fellowship and faith development happen.

3. *Spiritual Formation Groups* meet primarily for the purpose of personal faith development. These groups accent commitment and accountability in the context of the use of classical spiritual disciplines (prayer, meditation, Bible study, and service).

This type of group is well-known in Christian history. The Wesleyan Class or Band meeting embodies the genius of this model. These small groups emphasize personal accountability and growth in the context of a loving, supportive community.

David Watson has reapplied the Wesleyan model using many of the classical conventions:

127

* The group begins by developing a covenant that is specific and relevant to life.
* Each person agrees to attend regularly.
* Each person agrees not to leave the group without explanation.
* The group opens and closes with prayer.
* Each person relates to the group how he or she has succeeded or struggled with the group covenant in the past week (or relevant time period).[1]

The group covenant can cover whatever the group decides. The purpose is to encourage one another in carrying out this covenant through loving accountability.

The *Renovare* small group provides another expression of this type of group.[2] Richard Foster developed the *Renovare* groups as a means of encouraging personal and spiritual growth through small groups. The *Renovare* groups meet much like the covenant groups: they establish a group commitment, share progress on that commitment in the group, and then share prayer together. *Renovare* groups make more specific use of spiritual classics and the disciplines of prayer, meditation, and study; but otherwise parallel the covenant group model.

4. *Evangelistic Groups* structure themselves around the purpose of evangelism. The work of Paul Yonggi Cho in Korea has inspired many in other countries to emulate his cell-group process.[3] These groups are set up under the leadership of a lay pastor who is authorized and trained by the church staff. The group meeting includes prayer, praise and worship, Bible study, intercessory prayer, and the opportunity to make a profession of faith.[4] Most formats look something like this:

Introduction of New People	5-10 minutes
Worship/Singing/Testimonies	10-15 minutes
Bible Study with Application	30-60 minutes
Prayer and Consideration of New Prospects	10-15 minutes

A chair may be kept open in the room as a symbol of space available for new people. The format is intended both to teach those who are Christians and to invite in those who are not.[5]

Groups form most frequently according to location, taking place in the homes of the leaders.[6] The leader is responsible not only for the group meeting, but for visiting the members, and for inviting new people to the group. Every group is formed with the intention of both caring for existing believers and inviting others to faith. Groups expect to grow and finally to split into two groups. Each group has both a lay pastor and an assistant lay pastor. The latter will take the new group formed as the group reaches a certain level (normally sixteen to twenty) and become the lay pastor of that group. When the "cell" splits, two new assistants are chosen for each group, in preparation for future growth.

Cell groups exist to promote faith in nonbelievers and the growth of faith in believers. Cho's church prints a newspaper that provides curriculum for all of its cell groups, providing centralized content of the teaching. The staff of the church trains district leaders, who in turn train the individual cell group leader. The common curriculum and the hierarchical training of the leadership connect individual groups with the larger church.

5. *Therapeutic and Twelve Step Groups* meet to help people grow through personal crisis or pain or some range of needs. Many types of groups fall under this general umbrella. A support group might meet for people who have experienced a recent loss through death or divorce. Or the group might focus on dealing with specific personal issues for growth. Therapeutic or support groups differ from covenant groups in this specific focus on emotional and relationship issues, rather than more general personal and spiritual growth. Both, however, use the tools of accountability to the group as a means for personal growth.

The most popular type of therapeutic group right now is the Twelve-Step group.[7] The Twelve Step group uses the famous Twelve Steps of Alcoholics Anonymous and applies them to any sort of addictive or compulsive behavior. These groups encourage persons to face up honestly to their struggle, to confess their weakness, to learn to rely upon God, and to seek freedom from their addiction or compulsion one day at a time.

The group serves as a focus of both support and accountability.[8]

The Ingredients of an Effective Small Group

The expansion of small groups in churches in recent times does not mean that small groups are a panacea to all the church's needs. Small groups can frustrate as well as encourage. Early in our marriage, my wife and I were members of a group. The other couples were friends of ours, good and godly people. But after six months in that group we had to take a year off from any small group to recover. Why? Because the group neglected to do what it takes to make a small group effective.

A good small group begins with clear commitments. Groups succeed more frequently when the members of the group understand the commitment they are making. Unexpressed expectations destroy small groups. When people come into groups thinking that they will get certain needs met and the group neglects those needs, the group experience sours. When people come into groups and understand clearly what the group expects of them and what the group will and will not do for them, the group does well. Cohesion between small group members provides much of the power of the group to help people. Making the expectations and purpose of the group clear helps to build group unity.[9]

In our little group, each of the couples had different expectations, and we never agreed on a common purpose for the group. We would have done much better if we had begun with a group covenant that outlined what the group was intended to do, expectations for attendance and participation, and the basic structure of our times together. Some of our friends might have chosen not to come if we had done this, but that would have freed them to go to another group that would have met the needs they were seeking to address—instead of wasting six months waiting for our group to do what it never envisaged doing. Good groups begin with a clear statement of the purpose and expectations of the group.

Good groups have good leaders. Good groups do not just happen. Someone has to provide leadership. Our present-day emphasis on democratic process sometimes leads people to idealize small groups in which everyone leads, but too often groups in which "everyone leads" go nowhere.

Again, this was part of our small group's problem. No one was designated as our leader. Therefore, several of us vied for leadership and conflicted with one another. Those who did not try to lead resented those who did. No one had the ability even to try to help the group find a common ground. The result was frustration and chaos.

Leadership in small groups does not have to mean dominating the group. In fact, good leaders are typically democratic people who work at getting everyone involved and including people.

The group leader's job is the following:

* To help the group either understand or define its purpose and the commitment individuals make when they join the group.
* To keep the group faithful to these commitments so that the purpose remains alive.
* To make sure that everyone is able to participate in the group and has a chance to belong.
* To encourage the group and help the process of communication flow freely.
* To guard the group from people who would unconsciously dominate the group's time and unintentionally exclude others.
* To help the group evaluate its progress in keeping its commitments, and to judge when the group needs to change or quit altogether.[10]

Frequently, a good group leader has a pastoral dimension. This person calls those who are absent, welcomes those who are new, and mobilizes the group to meet needs. The leader may also be the teacher, although these roles can be separate.

Good leaders come in all shapes and sizes—male and female, old and young, with more or less education.[11] Good leaders have excellent people skills and Christian character worth emulating. They have the energy and time to devote to the task, and are willing to work with the church. Good small groups find leaders in many places, and provide many places for leadership development.

Good groups evaluate themselves. Groups experience difficulty when conflicts and expectations remain hidden and never discussed. Again, our group suffered because we never really talked about what we liked and did not like in the group.

Good evaluations bring everything out in the open. In one church the counseling groups go through regular and rigorous evaluations. Each person in the group fills out a form that asks probing questions—such as "Are the members of the group truly open and honest with one another?" "Does anyone tend to dominate the group?" "Does the leader perform her or his function well?"

A long, specific evaluation form is not strictly necessary. But at least every six months the group should ask itself, Is our purpose still the same? Are we following through on our commitments? Are we open and caring with one another? Are we interested in continuing, or should we stop the group? What do we need to do to make the group worthwhile for the future. Groups that avoid evaluation risk letting frustration build up and watching the effectiveness of the group slip away.

Good small groups are supported by the whole church. Small group programs succeed only where the whole church and the staff promote them wholeheartedly. This is especially true of the pastor. Public recognition and appreciation will energize the groups. Neglect will cause them to wither away.[12]

The churches with the most effective small group programs are those where small groups are the central organizing focus for all ministry with and to adults. When the central ministry and teaching function of the church grow primarily out of small groups, they thrive. Where small groups act as one of several programs, the groups are still effective, but it is harder to make them work. For this reason, churches tend to have either a large adult Sunday school or a large small-group program, but rarely both.

Drawbacks to Small Group Programs

Small groups do have negatives. They lose contact with the overall church more easily than adult classes, since they typically do not meet in the building. Churches cannot control small groups as easily as adult classes. Small groups foster lay independence, which may prove both good and bad. The loss of an occasional small group that goes its own way reflects the price of doing ministry through groups.

Small groups necessitate the development of more lay leadership. Churches currently strapped for leadership will have trouble imagining finding more leaders for small groups. In the long run, small groups create leadership. But short term, small groups may take leadership away from other programs.

Small groups also demand coordination. Churches that mobilize laity through small groups have to dedicate significant staff resources to maintaining communication and care for the group leaders. In the smaller church with one pastor, this means freeing the pastor from some tasks in order to facilitate the small groups.

Small groups represent a powerful tool for teaching and ministering to adults. The increasing number of models for small groups show that churches find life and energy in the small group. Small groups will have many successes and failures, but they cannot be ignored.

XII

TROUBLESHOOTING PROBLEMS IN ADULT CLASSES

If you are lucky, when problems come up in adult classes, the people involved will talk to the right leaders. However, most of the time, they do not. Church people typically do not take on problems directly. Therefore, church leaders need to learn to stay alert for signs of problems.

The old adage that "people vote with their feet" alerts us to be watchful. Disappearing people signifies an existing problem. Their absence will not define the problem, much less the solution, but leaving may be the only input you get.

Taking attendance helps locate problems in at least this sense: Growing classes suggest health, and shrinking classes sound the alarm. When the attendance virtually halved in a matter of two or three months, the Christian education director knew that something negative had happened. No one came to complain. No one seemed to be talking around the church. The people just disappeared. She recognized later that their slow response was part of the failure to rejuvenate the class. Everyone involved learned the lesson: watch class attendance as a signal of class health or the beginning of problems.

As well as watching the overall attendance, look at the attendance patterns of individuals. When steady members begin to miss, something is up. Sometimes this signals a problem in the life of the individual that has nothing to do with the class, but suggests a need for pastoral care (and in these cases the classes themselves are generally ahead in reaching out to the person). But other times, people drop out because of strains within the class that need attention. Often, the persons involved will not talk with church leadership unless asked.

Attendance patterns help locate problems. Next we need to define the problems and seek solutions. In general, adult classes face the following types of problems:

* Communication problems
* Financial problems
* Leadership problems
* Transitional problems

The types and variety of challenges that arise in an adult class go beyond the few simple suggestions we will make here, but a little foresight in these areas can avoid a significant amount of grief.

Communication Problems

Every year the Kingdom class had one major fundraiser. People donated items (from art to a week in a lake cabin), and the items were auctioned off to the members and a few friends. The class made it a fun night with food and entertainment. The evening was a crucial social and structural event for the class year.

One year this class event coincided with the annual church dinners that presented the program of the church and began the budget campaign. The adult classes normally play a major role in organizing and running the dinners. The Kingdom class found itself torn between the demands of its own major event and the church program. The church leaders felt frustrated that an important class "was not on board" for these critical dinners. The class felt that they were put in a situation where their major interests were being attacked by the church.

The problem reflects a classic failure of communication. No one had ever compared the church schedule with the class schedule (on either side). No one intentionally set out to make life difficult for anyone else, but it happened.

Failure to communicate has a high price tag. Hurt feelings cause problems in relationships long after the event has passed. In every church, communication—between the overall church and the individual class, between classes themselves, and within the class—can go awry and leave resentment, confusion, and a lack of confidence. Good communication between the church leadership and classes builds relationships and fosters cooperation.

What can you do? Communication always misses perfection, but the following guidelines can help.

Plan frequent meetings with class leaders. Meet at least quarterly with class leaders to discuss the overall church schedule and upcoming events. If a special event in the overall church life is near, schedule an additional meeting with classes to go over the event. These special and regular meetings allow classes and church leaders to share information, answer questions, hear complaints, and respond to needs. Frequent and regularly scheduled meetings between church leadership and class leadership help iron out problems as they happen and avoid others.

Publish your church's schedule of special events early and often. Reminding classes on a regular basis of the schedule of all-church events helps them to plan ahead without creating conflicts. One church publishes a yearly church calendar in June, and updates this regularly through the church newspaper.

Bring new class officers up to date quickly. Large churches may have a dozen or more classes, each with its own schedule of electing officers. Keeping new class officers up to date may be no small project. Consider creating a Handbook for Class Officers to outline the communication network that exists in the church for getting things done. The handbook should detail how to schedule classrooms for special events, how to get things published in the newspaper, how to arrange for child care, and how to relate to the financial secretary. When classes elect their new officers, the overall leader for adult education must send the new president the handbook. Having written guidelines in hand for basic church policy and procedures helps avoid many problems.

Classes should have their own methods for letting people know about schedules and procedures. Some classes have their own newsletters or use a phone chain for communication, but most follow some method of "getting the word out." On any given Sunday 15 to 25 percent of class members will be absent, so simply making an announcement does not suffice.

Financial Problems

A visitor in a small adult class saw the leader hold up two envelopes. "This," he said, "is for our missions projects." Holding up the other envelope, he said, "This goes to the church's Christian education program. Some of you wonder why we give a pledge and then to the Sunday school, too. But they get all over us if we don't put something in this envelope."

Just as money causes problems in churches, money can create conflict in adult classes, too. Classes naturally start handling their own money in order to do their own mission projects. This may include helping a person in the area who needs help (fixing up a house or buying needed groceries) and projects like supporting a missionary (especially someone related to the class). Classes respond enthusiastically to projects and people they know personally. This is good. But sometimes the class and the church structure can get crossed up over finances.

Individuals today view institutions suspiciously. Local churches tend to look at denominational structures and resent sending money "away" to unknown ends. But this same suspicion can exist within the congregation. People may be loyal to their adult class and wary of the "institutional" demands for support.

When the church tries to control the individual giving through the class, you can plan on frustration and resentment following. The leaders of the church become frustrated since they cannot control the money, and the class members resent their attempt.

The church best responds to the financial projects of classes by creating a sense of mutual cooperation. Ask classes to share their budgets with the adult education leadership, not for the purpose of controlling their spending, but for information. In turn, the church can share its resources with the class. If the class is involved in a missions project overseas, the church can share with them the information available through its resources on the project. Moreover, the church leadership should involve classes in all the financial decision making of the congregation. All classes can have representatives on the finance committee, on the missions council, and anywhere else the whole church decides on financial priorities. Many churches connect the fundraising campaign with adult classes. In this way, the fellowship network of the classes helps integrate people into the church-wide fundraising efforts.

The church can accept the benefits of the class and rejoice in the ministry each class does. Problems will not totally go away. The church structure (treasurer, senior pastor, and so on) will still wonder from time to time about how classes spend their money when the budgets are tight at church. But if the church owns and celebrates the ministry of the classes, the mutual goodwill this creates will work for the long-term benefit of the whole congregation.

Just as financial conflict can happen between the church and a class, financial decisions may also lead to problems *within* the class—especially when the class begins to help local people in need. Classes naturally respond to human need, and should. But this type of help poses several dangers:

* People with chronic need wear out a class.
* Unless there is widespread agreement on the way people are helped, some may begin to resent the process.
* People can take advantage of the class.
* The class may not be able to respond as generously to every need that comes along, setting up the appearance of favoritism.

A few safeguards can give classes room to respond to human need and avoid major problems:

Have a pre-set limit on any one gift to a person in need. If a family needs more than this, the class consults with a pastor. This helps avoid duplicating efforts, and enables the church to draw from a greater number of families where necessary.

Have people bring appeals for financial needs to the class officers and not directly to the class. Bringing a need for even a good cause to a class puts the class in a difficult position. The timing may be wrong, but who wants to reject the impassioned plea of a friend? A mutual agreement to allow only projects and needs brought through the class officers or committee for these events helps avoid putting unfair pressure on people.

Leadership Problems

Leadership makes or breaks an adult class. Dealing with a problem in leadership challenges the most adroit church politician. Some people make poor class presidents, but they want to be president anyway. Good people can have problems in leadership roles. They may be too reserved, or they may so sincerely believe in something that they chase away everyone who is not as zealous as themselves. Their intentions may not be bad, but the results remain the same: people stay away when they feel uncomfortable.

No one can ensure that classes will always choose good leaders. Classes can make sure that they follow a fair method of selecting leaders, that they make a real attempt to match the needs of the position with the ability of the people, and that responsibility is shared. A good process for selecting leaders helps avoid many problems.

Develop a clear procedure for electing or nominating leaders, and clear job descriptions. Nominating committees work wonders for putting people in good jobs. So long as the membership of the nominating committee itself rotates and the procedure runs the same for everyone, most classes experience only rare complaints about favoritism.

Allow a variety of people to share in the up-front running of the class. Many classes have one person lead the class, another handle music, another handle prayer, and perhaps another introduce newcomers. If the main leader handles the flow well, this gives a sense of belonging to a larger number of people, and ego problems are held in check.

Rotate officers every election. Most people prefer to serve at most one year in any office, and many classes opt for six-month terms. More frequent changes than every six months probably means that the officers will never have the chance to develop any ideas. But changing officers at least annually keeps people fresh and willing and more effective.

Intervene rarely, but when necessary. When significant problems appear, the pastor or appropriate leader should intervene in a class to deal with a leadership problem. Situations do arise where a person creates problems that threaten to destroy the class. In these cases no easy answers exist, and no painless solution will present itself. Nevertheless, the leadership of the church has to intervene and deal with the problem for the sake of the class.

Transitional Problems

Classes go through changes, and not all changes help. We always faced a crisis when our newlywed class turned into a young parents class. When this necessitated the formation of another newlywed class, the former newlywed class always went through a frustrating time. Suddenly, they no longer received the influx of young couples and the easy growth that came with helping the newly married. At the same time, many of the families in the class became more erratic in their attendance due to the extra illness and fatigue that comes with newborn babies. Attendance usually dropped, and with it the morale of the class. At this time, the class needed encouragement and guidance from the church leaders.

Classes experience change and transition for many different reasons:

* Classes age and begin to lose members to health problems or death.
* Economic hard times cause classes to suffer when members experience layoffs or moves forced by economics.
* Singles classes change as people marry or move.
* Families within the classes change through death or divorce, and the relationships within the classes undergo change.

Each type of change causes its own problems within a class. Good help from the pastor or church leadership can help classes deal with the change and go on.

The church can help classes anticipate times of transition and explain what is going on. Classes benefit from knowing that what they are experiencing comes from the normal life cycle and not from their own failure. Otherwise, a class can easily interpret a loss of momentum as rejection and personal failure. Take time to explain to classes what is happening. Learn to anticipate some of the changes and share with the class before it happens. Begin newlywed classes by explaining the natural transition into "the young parents' class," with the hope that they will be ready when it happens.

The church can help a class interpret change positively. When the Circle class reached its sixtieth anniversary, we threw them a party and thanked them for their years of devotion. We realized that we were seeing these loved saints at the end of their lives, and we celebrated their lifetimes of service.

The Koinonia class succeeded wonderfully in drawing together young singles for about five years. Then, the leadership married or moved. Over time, the class disappeared and another class was started. That class, too, was successful and then went through decline. The singles began to wonder, "What are we doing wrong?" We learned to tell them, "You did nothing wrong. You helped people find good Christian mates and develop their faith before moving on in their jobs. People change, and you were a positive part of that change. But you cannot stop change. Your very decline reflects your success in creating a good place for single adults." We thus learned to celebrate the good work of a class however long the life cycle of the class was.

The church can provide special courses that reflect the transition through which the class is going. One church, hard hit by the economic problems, created courses that dealt with the topic of faith and tough times. This follows the general desire to build practical courses that address the felt needs of people. Other churches in the midst of the economic struggles of their members developed courses in budgeting, reducing debt, and other general financial topics. Some of these were special courses, and some were worked into the Sunday morning curriculum. Sensitivity to the transitions of the classes helps to keep all facets of the educational ministry of the church relevant and helpful.

This attempt at troubleshooting does not begin to cover all the possible challenges adult classes can throw at the church. The root of all of what we have said remains the same: listen to people and respond to their needs. Classes do a marvelous job of taking care of their members. A little forethought and help goes a long way in easing the classes through troubled times back into fruitful ministry.

NOTES

1. WHO NEEDS ADULT CLASSES, ANYWAY?

1. Lyle Schaller, "From Older and Smaller to Younger and Larger: The Road to Redevelopment," *Net Results* 10 (October 1991): 7.

2. *Effective Christian Education: A National Study of Protestant Congregations—a Report for The United Methodist Church* (Minneapolis: Search Institute, 1990), p. 61.

3. Warren J. Hartman and Robert L. Wilson, *The Large Church Membership* (Nashville: Discipleship Resources, 1989), p. 25.

4. Dr. James B. Buskirk is the Senior Pastor of First United Methodist Church in Tulsa, Oklahoma. He previously served as Dean of the Graduate School of Theology, Oral Roberts University, and before that was Professor of Evangelism, Candler School of Theology. See also George Hunter, *The Contagious Congregation* (Nashville: Abingdon Press, 1979), pp. 28-30.

5. See the discussion on Bonhoeffer's concept of "silence" in Dietrich Bonhoeffer, *Worldly Preaching: Lectures on Homiletics*, ed. and trans. by Clyde E. Fant (New York: Crossroads, 1991), pp. 52-53.

6. Win Arn, "Mass Evangelism: The Bottom Line," in Win Arn, ed., *The Pastor's Church Growth Handbook* (Pasadena, Calif.: Church Growth Press, 1979), p. 102.

7. Dietrich Bonhoeffer, *Life Together* (San Francisco: Harper and Bros., 1954), p. 23.

8. Lawrence M. Brammer, *The Helping Relationship: Process and Skills*, 3rd ed. (Englewood Cliffs, N.J.: Prentice-Hall, 1985), p. 16. Brammer points to the success of self-help groups in this way. Peer-relationships, encouragement and accountability help people make changes in their lives in dealing with problems from alcoholism to overeating.

9. This is the main point of the groups proposed by David Lowes Watson in *Accountable Discipleship: Handbook for Covenant Discipleship Groups in the Congregation* (Nashville: Discipleship Resources, 1984).

10. The example here was given to me by Tom Albin.

11. Carl A. Volz, *Pastoral Life and Practice in the Early Church* (Minneapolis: Augsburg Fortress, 1990), pp. 82-87.

2. THE GROWING BUSINESS OF ADULT LEARNING

1. Stephen D. Brookfield, *Understanding and Facilitating Adult Learning* (San Francisco: Jossey-Bass, 1986), p. 242. Brookfield notes that "extension workers are more likely to conform to their employer's expectations than to those of their clientele." When you think about it, this is not very surprising—people respond most quickly to those who control their employment. But what does this suggest for the church? There will be a natural tendency for the church to pay attention to those who are already *in* the church or to denominational officials who control movement between positions, rather than to unchurched people who might be influenced to join the church.

2. For a variety of analyses on this point, see ibid., chapter 2; Huey B. Long, "Understanding Adult Learners" in Michael W. Galbraith, ed., *Adult Learning Methods* (Malabar, Fla.: Krieger Publishing Company, 1990), pp. 23-38; Malcolm Knowles, *The Adult Learner: A Neglected Species*, 4th ed. (Houston: Gulf Publishing Company, 1990), chapter 3.

3. Huey B. Long, *Adult Learning: Research and Practice* (New York: Cambridge, The Adult Learning Company, 1983), pp. 98-100.

4. Ibid., p. 103.

5. U. Bergston, "Interest in Education Among Adults with Short Previous Formal Schooling," *Adult Education* 30, 3: 131-51.

6. Long, *Adult Learning: Research and Practice*, pp. 88-96; Brookfield, *Understanding and Facilitating Adult Learning*, p. 5.

7. A. H. Maslow, *Motivation and Personality*, 2nd ed. (New York: Harper & Row, 1970).

8. Long, *Adult Learning: Research and Practice*, p. 184.

9. From a lecture by George Barna, "Discovering the New World," at the Leadership Network Conference, *The Church in the Twenty-first Century* (Denver, Colo.: August 20, 1991).

10. This is especially the point of adult learning theory which flows out of so-called "liberal adult education theory"; for a summary see John L. Elias and Sharan Merriam, *Philosophical Foundations of Adult Education* (Malabar, Fla.: Robert E. Krieger Publishing, 1980), pp. 62-64.

11. Knowles, *The Adult Learner: A Neglected Species*, p. 41; Elias and Merriam, *Philosophical Foundations of Adult Education*, pp. 115-27.

12. Obviously many adult educators who are not necessarily from a Christian viewpoint would agree with this. See Brookfield, *Understanding and Facilitating Adult Learning*, pp. 21-24.

3. CLASSES HAVE PERSONALITIES

1. See "Tulsa Shoppers: Ambassadors for America," *American Demographics* (January 1992): 12-15, for a description of how people prefer to shop.

2. There are other factors that affect the nature of individual adult classes, especially considerations of generation and social and economic life-styles. We will not deal with these here, but see Lyle E. Schaller, *Reflections of a Contrarian: Second Thoughts on the Parish Ministry* (Nashville: Abingdon Press, 1989), pp. 65-95 for a good description of generational differences between groups within the church; and Tex Sample, *U.S. Lifestyles and Mainline Churches: A Key to Reaching People in the 90's* (Louisville: Westminster/John Knox Press, 1990) for a discussion of cultural life-style differences within the church.

3. Isabel B. Myers, *Introduction to Type*, 3rd ed. (Palo Alto, Calif.: Consulting Psychologists Press, 1980). Classes, of course, being collections of people are more complex even than individuals. My assumption based on unscientific observation is that similar individuals tend to get together in classes, so that we can organize our observations of classes as I have done in this chapter.

4. See Warren J. Hartman, *Five Audiences: Identifying Groups in Your Church* (Nashville: Abingdon Press, 1987). Hartman's approach is statistically and empirically based, while my approach is more psychological, experiential, and anecdotal. Both approaches have merit and insight, and both have limitations. But together they serve to underline the real tendency of people to group together according to similarities that are important to them.

5. Note Hartman's description of the "Fellowship" oriented class, *Five Audiences: Identifying Groups in Your Church*, pp. 29-40. However, since all classes are in some sense fellowship oriented, I think it makes more sense to see these people as extroverted and social in personality.

6. Ibid. Hartman calls this the "social action" group, pp. 68-73. As he admits (p. 73) this in younger people can be combined with theologically conservative views. In my opinion, the connection between liberal theology and the older members of this group is less significant than the drive to service and practical application that comes from their personality. I suspect that the differences in generations here reflect the tendency to approach faith as a reenforcement for their desire for action rather than as a motivator for that action.

7. See ibid., p. 96; figure 1. For this group the most important quality of the teacher by far is that they, "show love and concern about people." I suspect that for this group "showing love" is not merely a verbal expression of concern, but stresses concrete and visible action.

8. Ibid., pp. 49-54.

9. Again, see the chart in ibid., p. 96.

10. See Daniel J. Levinson, *The Seasons of a Man's Life* (New York: Ballantine Books, 1978).

11. For a good summary see Douglas C. Kimmel, *Adulthood and Aging*, 2nd ed. (New York: John Wiley and Sons, 1980). See especially chapter 1. James F. Cobble, Jr., *Faith and Crisis in the Stages of Life* (Peabody, Mass.: Hendrickson Publishing, 1985) is helpful for those trying to understand the implications of one's stage in life for the church.

12. George E. Vaillant, *Adaptation to Life* (Boston: Little, Brown and Company, 1977), p. 216; also Kimmel, *Adulthood and Aging*, p. 97.

13. Levinson, *The Seasons of a Man's Life*, pp. 98-101.

14. Kimmel, *Adulthood and Aging*, pp. 203-6.

15. See Vaillant, *Adaptation to Life*, pp. 216-19. Vaillant notes, "The excitement and potential excellence of the college sample became now lost in conformity. Men who at nineteen had radiated charm now seemed colorless, hardworking, bland young men in 'gray flannel suits' " (p. 217).

16. Gail Sheehy's book, *Passages: Predictable Crisis of Adult Life* (New York: E. P. Dutton and Company, 1976), promotes the crisis concept through her anecdotal presentation. But Vaillant, *Adaptation to Life*, p. 223, found little evidence for the crisis notion. Progression, growth, and change were there, but not dramatic crisis as a rule.

17. Kimmel, *Adulthood and Aging*, pp. 102-4.

4. FORMING NEW ADULT CLASSES

1. Dick Murray, *Strengthening the Adult Sunday School Class* (Nashville: Abingdon Press, 1981), pp. 66-70. Murray lists two myths about adult classes "Class time around the coffee pot is wasted" and "Adult classes are stronger with few social events." These are myths because they reflect an attitude that pretends adult classes in a church are primarily for learning. In fact, it is the social function of the class that is primary.

2. Lyman Coleman's material on groups offers a wide selection of conversation starters. See Lyman Coleman, *Encyclopedia of Serendipity* (Littleton, Colo.: Serendipity House, 1980). Some further resources can be found in the training material for small group leaders provided by Judy Hamlin, *The Small Group Leaders Training Course* (Colorado Springs, Colo.: NavPress, 1990).

5. RECRUITING TEACHERS IS EASIER THAN TRAINING THEM

1. See George Barna's discussion of the approach of people toward commitment in *The Frog in the Kettle: What Christians Need to Know About Life in the Year 2000* (Ventura, Calif.: Regal Books, 1990), pp. 33-35.

2. See Patricia Braus, "What Workers Want," *American Demographics* 14 (August 1992): 36.

3. Marlene Wilson, *The Effective Management of Volunteer Programs* (Boulder, Colo.: Volunteer Management Associates, 1976). See especially chapter 3, "Motivation: The Whys of Behavior," pp. 41-74.

4. See Dick Murray, *Strengthening the Adult Sunday School Class* (Nashville: Abingdon Press, 1981), pp. 89-100. Murray debunks the myth that lectures are poor or manipulative methods of teaching.

5. For more on evaluation of volunteers, see Wilson, *The Effective Management of Volunteer Programs*, pp. 87-91.

6. Stephen D. Brookfield, *Understanding and Facilitating Adult Learning* (San Francisco: Jossey-Bass Publishers, 1986), pp. 133-35.

7. Warren Hartman notes slight differences between types of classes and what they prefer in teachers. See *Five Audiences: Identifying Groups in Your Church* (Nashville: Abingdon Press, 1987), pp. 95-103. As he notes, the Traditionalist group will place the highest value on Bible knowledge, while a social-action group will not worry as much about this. All groups, however, value teachers they respect who show love and concern for them as individuals.

8. On discussions, see Murray, *Strengthening the Adult Sunday School Class*, pp. 94-100.

6. CUSTOM-FIT CURRICULUM

1. See Stephen D. Brookfield, *Understanding and Facilitating Adult Learning* (San Francisco: Jossey-Bass Publishers, 1986), p. 246, on arranging courses around problem solving.

2. Ibid., pp. 246-48. See also, James Michael Lee, *The Flow of Religious Instruction* (Birmingham: Religious Education Press, 1973), pp. 230-68.

3. A more exhaustive and technical bibliographical source for Bible study, *Biblical Resources for Ministry*, is available through the Asbury Theological Seminary bookstore, Asbury Theological Seminary, 204 N. Lexington Avenue, Wilmore, KY 40390.

4. For more on interpretive questions see Robert A. Traina, *Methodological Bible Study: A New Kind of Hermeneutical Manual* (Grand Rapids: Francis Asbury Press, 1980), pp. 97-135. A simpler form of this approach can be found in David Thompson, *Bible Study That Works* (Grand Rapids: Francis Asbury Press, 1982).

7. ADULT LEARNING OPPORTUNITIES OTHER THAN SUNDAY

1. For a more complete description of this type of church, see Lyle E. Schaller, *The Seven-Day-A-Week Church* (Nashville: Abingdon Press, 1992), especially, chapters 1, 3, and 4.

2. *Precepts* Bible studies are produced by Precepts Ministries, P.O. Box 182218, Chattanooga, TN 37422-7218. Nellie M. Moser, ed., *Disciple: Becoming Disciples Through Bible Study*, Study Manual (Nashville: Graded Press, 1987).

3. Course material for this is provided for by Bruce L. Bugbee Networking (Charles E. Fuller Institute, P.O. Box 91990, Pasadena, CA 91109-1990).

4. Information from a discussion with Rick Warren in June 1992 and from a talk given by Rick Warren at "The Church in the Twenty-first Century" conference in Dallas, Texas on June 17, 1992. This talk, "A Vision for the Whole," is available through Convention Cassettes Unlimited, 41-550 Eclectic Street, Suite C-140, Palm Desert, CA 92260.

8. ADULT LEARNING IN THE SMALL CHURCH

1. See Ronald H. Cram, "The Small Membership Church: Recent Trends in Research and Program" in Nancy T. Folz, *Religious Education in the Small Membership Church* (Birmingham: The Religious Education Press, 1990), p. 59; and Gary E. Farley, "Understanding the Sociological Perspective," idem., pp. 76-80; Lyle E. Schaller, *The Small Church Is Different!* (Nashville: Abingdon Press, 1982), pp. 17-55.

2. The preceding observations come from Dr. Ron Crandall, Professor of Evangelism at Asbury Theological Seminary. I am thankful to Dr. Crandall for his time and comments on the subject of this chapter.

3. In 1988, 58 percent said they would "definitely," "probably," or "possibly" go to church. Only 37 percent said they would "definitely" or "probably" not return to church. See George Gallup, Jr., and Jim Castelli, *The People's Religion: American Faith in the 1990s* (New York: Macmillan, 1989), p. 140.

4. Ibid., p. 145.

5. Richard Beckhard, *Changing the Essence: The Art of Creating and Leading Fundamental Change in Organizations* (San Francisco: Jossey-Bass Publishers, 1992), p. 75.

6. Steve Burt, *Activating Leadership in the Small Church: Clergy and Laity Working Together.* (Valley Forge, Pa.: Judson Press, 1988), p. 47.

7. Holsinger and Laycock would *require* the pastor to become "the chief Christian educator of the local congregation" (James W. Holsinger, Jr., and Evelyn Laycock, *Awaken the Giant: 28 Prescriptions for*

NOTES

Reviving The United Methodist Church [Nashville: Abingdon Press, 1989], pp. 138-39). Lyle Schaller, *The Small Church Is Different* (p. 120) also makes this recommendation.

9. ROOMS AND EQUIPMENT FOR ADULT LEARNING

1. Lyle Schaller, *Reflections of a Contrarian: Second Thoughts on the Parish Ministry* (Nashville: Abingdon Press, 1989), p. 115.
2. According to George Barna, *The Frog in the Kettle: What Christians Need to Know About Life in the Year 2000* (Ventura, Calif.: Regal Books, 1990), p. 61.
3. Resources for the use of media in the church include Robert Heinich, Michael Molenda, and James D. Russell, *Instructional Media and the New Technologies of Instruction*, 3rd ed. (New York: Macmillan, 1989); Ronald A. Sarno, *Using Media in Religious Education* (Birmingham: Religious Education Press, 1987); *The Equipment Directory of Video, Computer, and Audio-Visual Products, 1991–1992*, 37th ed. (Fairfax, Va.: The International Communications Industries Association, 1991); *The Video Source Book, 1993*, 14th ed. (Detroit: Gale Research 1993).

10. SINGLE CLASSES ARE DIFFERENT—AND NOT

1. According to George Barna (*The Frog in the Kettle: What Christians Need to Know About Life in the Year 2000* [Ventura, Calif.: Regal Books, 1990], p. 67), in 1990 the median age for first marriage was 25.9 years for men and 23.6 years for women. In 1960 the median age for men was 22.8 years, and 20.3 years for women.
2. Statistics taken from George Barna, *What Americans Believe: An Annual Survey of Values and Religious Views in the United States* (Ventura, Calif.: Regal Books, 1991), chapters 19-21, and also the charts on pages 47 and 88.
3. Ibid., p. 47.
4. Ibid., p. 280.
5. Ibid., p. 273.
6. See also the statistics put together in Harold Ivan Smith, "Singles Ministry Cannot Be Ignored," pp. 18-20, and Dennis Franck, "Singles Ministries Meet Needs," pp. 20-21, both in Jerry Jones, ed., *Singles Adult Ministry* (Colorado Springs, Colo.: NavPress, 1991).
7. Douglas W. Johnson, *The Challenge of Singles Adult Ministry* (Valley Forge, Pa.: Judson Press, 1982), pp. 94-98.
8. For an excellent book on the program and structure of the large singles class (following the Christ United Methodist Church of Tulsa,

Oklahoma, experience) see Harry Odum, *The Vital Singles Ministry*, Effective Church Series (Nashville: Abingdon Press, 1992). I am also indebted to an interview with the Senior Pastor of Christ United Methodist, Dr. Robert Pierson, for the information on this excellent group.

9. See James Richwine, "Selecting and Training Singles Leaders," in Jones, ed., *Singles Adult Ministry*, pp. 80-86 who also stresses the importance of both male and female leaders for singles.

10. I was greatly helped in this chapter through an interview with Mary Randolph, Director of Singles, Asbury United Methodist Church, Tulsa, Oklahoma.

11. SMALL GROUPS FOR ADULT LEARNING

1. David Watson, *Accountable Discipleship* (Nashville: Discipleship Resources, 1983), p. 60.

2. *Renovare*, P.O. Box 879, Wichita, KS 67201-0879. *Renovare* provides a *Spiritual Formation Workbook* by James B. Smith to facilitate these groups.

3. Paul Yonggi Cho, *Successful Home Cell Groups* (South Plainfield, N.J.: Bridge Publishing, 1981).

4. See the diagrams provided in Lyman Coleman, *Serendipity Training Manual* (Littleton, Colo.: Serendipity House, 1987), pp. 46-49.

5. See also the tapes and training materials from Dan Reiland, *Starting Small Groups in Your Church* (El Cajon, Calif.: INJOY, 1991).

6. However, see the "Small Group Seminar" material of New Hope Community Church in Portland, Oregon, that also has specialized groups that serve singles, remarrieds, youth, and those involved in different ministries. The purely geographical division of groups (normally by Zip Codes) can be modified in this way.

7. Note the comments of George Hunter, *How to Reach Secular People* (Nashville: Abingdon Press, 1992), pp. 63-64. Hunter sees Twelve-Step groups as one of the most significant tools for reaching secular people at this time.

8. For resources in applying the Twelve Steps to a broader and specifically Christian context see Friends in Recovery Staff, *The Twelve Steps—A Spiritual Journey: A Working Guide for Adult Children from Addictive and Other Dysfunctional Families* (San Diego, Calif.: Recovery Publications, Inc., 1988); Dr. Bill Lantz, *Workbook for Christian Twelve Steps Groups*, privately published, c/o First United Methodist Church, 1115 So. Boulder, Tulsa, OK 74119.

9. Nathan W. Turner, *Effective Leadership in Small Groups* (Valley Forge, Pa.: Judson Press, 1977), p. 11; Malcolm Knowles and Hulda Knowles, *Introduction to Group Dynamics: What It Is, Its Main Ideas, Its*

Language, Its Applications, 2nd ed. (New York; Association Press, 1972), pp. 58-59.

10. See Turner, *Effective Leadership in Small Groups,* pp. 11-12.

11. Dr. Cho's enormous church grew through the primary use of women as the cell leaders, even though Korea was hardly a liberated country in terms of women's roles. For his description of this phenomenon, see Cho, *Successful Home Cell Groups,* pp. 24ff. Women leaders also outnumbered men in the early Wesleyan movement, see Paul Chilcotte, "The Women Pioneers of Early Methodism," in Theodore Runyon, ed., *Wesleyan Theology Today: A Bicentennial Theological Consultation* (Nashville: Kingswood Books, 1985), pp. 180-84. The point is to be open to leadership wherever you find it in persons.

12. Cho makes this point in his book, *Successful Home Group Cells,* pp. 136-43, as does Alvin F. Zander, *Making Groups Effective* (San Francisco: Jossey-Bass Publishers, 1982) p. 128. Public support of groups facilitates the effectiveness of the group.

Printed in the United States
1520